Mademoiselle

BRUNO

MONSAINGEON

Mademoiselle

conversations with
Nadia Boulanger

translated by Robyn Marsack

NORTHEASTERN UNIVERSITY PRESS

Boston

First Northeastern University Press edition 1988

First published in Great Britain in 1985 by Carcanet Press Limited, 208–212 Corn Exchange, Manchester, M4 3BQ

Translation © Robyn Marsack 1985
Mademoiselle: Entretiens avec Nadia Boulanger was first published in France by Editions Van de Velde, 1981.

Library of Congress Cataloging-in-Publication Data

Monsaingeon, Bruno.
   Mademoiselle: Conversations with Nadia Boulanger.

   Translation of: Mademoiselle.
   Includes index.
   Discography: p.
   1. Boulanger, Nadia. 2. Music teachers—Biography.
I. Boulanger, Nadia. II. Title.
ML423.B52M613   1988   780'.92'4 [B]   87–28307
ISBN   1–55553–026–5

Printed and bound by Alpine Press, Stoughton, Massachusetts. The paper is 55# Rivertone Cream, an acid-free sheet.

MANUFACTURED IN THE UNITED STATES OF AMERICA

91 90 89 88 87 5 4 3 2 1

Contents

Acknowledgements

Let me thank here those who have made an invaluable contribution to the book: Leonard Bernstein, Lennox Berkeley, Hugues Cuenod, Yehudi Menuhin, Jeremy Menuhin, Murray Perahia and Pierre Schaeffer, who responded so touchingly to my requests by sending me their personal recollections of Nadia Boulanger.

And then my father, André Monsaingeon, who put considerable work into the preparation of the raw material, which was my starting point in developing the book; and Gabrielle Gugenheim Babin, who sustained me in my undertaking by her conviction — without their persuasion this book would not have seen the light of day.

Except for the photographs on pp. 18, 19, 22, 117 by Patrick Guis, and on p. 119 by Roger Picard (courtesy of Radio France), the photographs were made available through the kindness of Annette Dieudonné.

Translator's note

I should like to add my thanks to Elliott Carter, for summoning his memories at short notice, and to Doda Conrad, who kindly provided an extract from his memoirs. For their most helpful advice and criticism, I am indebted to Bruno Monsaingeon, Marilynn Phillips, Michael Schmidt and Stuart Airlie; also to W. J. Strachan, who translated the tribute from Pierre Schaeffer.

This book was first given to me by Nicole Jordan, and it is to her that this translation is dedicated. In Nadia Boulanger's words: *Il n'est pas triste d'avoir à donner.*

Author's Note

These conversations with Nadia Boulanger obviously never took place, at least not in the form and with the structure in which they are presented here. However, there is nothing in what follows that is not hers. In the course of the five years of our intermittent encounters — those were the last years of her life — there was no possibility of creating a script with Nadia Boulanger. One does not direct a woman of her age and stature: between her eighty-sixth and ninety-first years, each day she had uncomplainingly surrendered more of her body to the earth, so there must have seemed very little left for death to claim, but her spirit remained indomitable.

This is not the place to exaggerate the importance of my task, but to give an account of its difficulties, which to some extent explain the inevitable limits of the final product.

The writing of this book was very much akin to editing a film, whose scenario would have been written after the shooting. But the existence of such a film depends on preliminary sequences shot with the leading actor. If the latter dies before the shooting is over, nothing remains for the director but to undertake a new shooting or to find a twin. By comparison with these technical impasses, writing has more than one advantage.

In order to cover for those sequences and linking scenes that were missing, what I had to do — by an effort of identification with the main character, by an attempt to penetrate her mind through what I knew were her essential preoccupations — was to discover in writing a stylistic twin of Nadia Boulanger.

By allowing myself this liberty, I could proceed further and perhaps enrich the material, limited by its very materiality — the sound of recorded words — which had been formerly and partially the subject of two processes: one for a film on Mademoiselle, the other for a series of radio interviews with her.

I have never been particularly fond of puzzles, and the business of reorganizing scattered thoughts, even when they are the expression of intuitions that are dazzling, Pascalian, as was the case with those of Nadia Boulanger, had no appeal for me unless it contributed to something more: making perceptible in a different medium the strength and savour of a person who exercised a major influence on musical life in the twentieth century. It involved re–creating on paper, even to imperfections in syntax, her style and emotion. It is in this style, semi–conversational, semi–formal, that those — innumerable — who knew her will find, I hope, the thought of Nadia Boulanger, as she herself would have expressed it.

I held to a respect for authenticity and even when I would have liked to see her develop a subject more substantially before abruptly branching off, refused on principle to shackle an often impulsive personality. Moreover, Nadia Boulanger did not care to confide things, either about herself or about others, which those more shrewd or more relentless than I was would eventually have been able to extract from her. Such was not my aim. This accounts for the absence of many names of people who were nevertheless important to her; of many subjects, similarly, which she would probably have been willing to explore some thirty years earlier and which she does not even touch upon in this book. Hence its limitations, which I willingly abstained from overstepping, in a manner which would necessarily have been arbitrary.

The form of a dialogue, which I finally retained, was not an *a priori* necessity. It simply seemed to me the most plausible and the most workable. I nevertheless tried to restrict it where possible, reintegrating most of my questions into her own speech and utilising them openly only where links were necessary.

Bruno Monsaingeon
Paris 1981

Introduction

The extraordinary human and moral radiance resulting from her intense dedication to music comes through even in these interviews, given by Nadia Boulanger in her late eighties when she was almost totally blind and quite infirm. Her ability to carry on in spite of terrible physical drawbacks, and to talk as she had so often to students throughout her life, are examples of what every student was aware of — that dedication to her art and her students which absorbed all her attention.

I remember the day in, I think, 1934, when the Stavisky affair caused rioting in the Place de la Concorde, stopped the metro, and made it perilous to walk the streets of Paris because of various rioting mobs. I walked from my hotel on the left bank to the Ecole Normale, a walk of several miles through a terrifying Paris, to a counterpoint lesson. A few other students prudently did not show up, but Mademoiselle was there, and with a melancholy smile announced that music must go on, no matter what.

Some of this indomitable character comes through in the remarks in this book, remarks which every one of her vast number of English, American, Polish, South American, French and other students will recognize as I do. What does not come across, of course, is the personal situation of a lesson, which brought out the remarks so aptly that they were never forgotten. In fact, each seemed so pointed, so important and so meaningful to a student that it comes as a surprise to find that many of these must have been repeated often, and were part of a repertory of remarks. For at the time each was said, it was so appropriate and seemed so spontaneous, as if thought up on the spur of the moment. Yet reading this book is for me like being at a lesson once again, except that many of the very precise technical matters we discussed and evaluated are omitted. So are the changing moods of those times when Mademoiselle was at her best, when she was by turns deeply serious or humorously teasing to arouse us to some kind of action. Here, in old age, her talk is understandably most serious and somewhat melancholy, moods which were not so prevalent in her earlier years.

In the language of today, it would be said that Nadia Boulanger was exceptionally charismatic, and indeed often seemed to dominate those who would not stand up to her, but it was not these qualities which made her important to so many musicians. For what was really valuable was that she made the art of music itself charismatic. She showed how many-sided, how all-embracing, devotion to it could be. Paul Valéry called Mademoiselle 'la musique en personne' (music in person), but for us she made music a person — to be much loved, cherished, taken care of, devoting our greatest attentiveness and respect to it, wanting to make ourselves worthy of this wonderful art.

This book gives a partial impression of this aspect of her teaching and her contacts with us, unlike any of the biographies I have read. For such a person, the narrative of her comings and goings, successes and mistakes, only touches the surface; these interviews help those who did not know her to understand something of what made her such a great teacher, with a widespread influence on many performers and especially on contemporary composers. In the early 1920s she taught a whole generation of American composers, among them Herbert Elwell, Aaron Copland, Roy Harris, Walter Piston, Theodore Chanler and Virgil Thomson. Thus she changed the face of American music, and established a reputation that continued to draw students to her until her death in 1979.

Elliott Carter
Rome, 1985

Overture à la Française

Aaron Copland, one of your most famous pupils, wrote in Harpers
Magazine *(1960): 'It is now almost forty years since I first rang the bell at
Nadia Boulanger's Paris apartment and asked her to accept me as her
composition pupil. Any young musician may do the same thing today, for
Mademoiselle Boulanger lives at the same address, in the same apartment, and teaches with the same formidable energy. The only difference
is that she was then comparatively little-known outside the Parisian
musical world, and today there are few musicians anywhere who would
not concede her to be the most famous of living composition teachers.'*

*It seems to me that this description, given eighteen years ago, exactly
establishes the context in which we find ourselves now.*

Yes, the apartment is the same, but have I ever been as he
describes? I venture to doubt it, because I believe that a teacher
depends on the quality of his students, and that his role is a little
less grand, less omnipotent than one would like people to think.

But let's accept Copland's customary kindness. He was here in
1921 as a young man, and then became in the following years a
really good friend with whom I still keep in touch.

I was born in 1887. My parents moved house at a time I can't
recall because I was too small, and we lived in the rue La Bruyère
until 1904. And since 1904 we have been here amongst the
furniture that my grandmother had, I swear this is the truth . . .
in 1835. These are therefore souvenirs of incomparable significance for me. I think it is because of that — I know how much I
have changed, I know how much I have aged – people tell me,
'you haven't changed.' I think that it's because I've never wanted
to follow fashion, I've never altered my clothes. I have almost the
same ones, the furniture is the same. So amidst all these sur-
roundings people see me as I have always been, but maybe
another person is here now, and they don't register the difference

because of what has persisted despite change. I love the unchanging in all things.

Marie Julie Boulanger, paternal grandmother of Nadia Boulanger. Born: 1786. Debut: 1811, as mezzo-soprano at the Opéra-Comique in a work by Gretry. First prize at the Conservatoire: 1812.
Ernest Boulanger, father of Nadia Boulanger. Born: 1815. Prix de Rome: 1835.
Nadia Boulanger. Born: 1887. Prix du Conservatoire 1904. Prix de Rome: 1908.
Lili Boulanger, her sister. Born: 1893. Grand Prix de Rome: 1913.

My father could have known Beethoven. He was born sixty-five years after the death of Bach, twelve years before the death of Beethoven, and he knew Paris in the great century of Romanticism.

He was an extraordinarily approachable and open man, but he never talked about himself, and when he died I was only twelve. He took part in our great aesthetic discussions. I know little things, I know of his adoration for his mother because we often went to the cemetery — to the one in which the tomb lies where I will join them one day. It was of the utmost importance to him to take his little bouquet to his mother.

Your father was the musical element in the family?

Everyone was musical, more or less, because my mother was an amateur but true artist, although she never thought of creating anything; she got married very young, and afterwards gave her life entirely, day and night, to us. All that I have been able to do more or less decently in life, I owe to her influence, to her exceptional intelligence. Much as she adored me, she knew how to be severe, demanding not just some attention but *all* possible attention. She showed this in a way that strikes a chord in me to this day. We were leaving the Conservatoire and I was not exactly subdued, having come first. . . . The teachers surrounded me with a kind of legend passed down from my father, who had left an extraordinary impression on all of them; in short, a combination of things conspired to give me virtues I didn't have, powers I didn't possess; but my mother was never fooled. She was absolutely indifferent to my being first. And that day she said to me: 'Yes, all that is very nice, but tell me, do you reckon you have done all you are capable of?' And when she said *all*, I understood and I understand it today, that I haven't done all I could. I have worked hard, but I haven't done everything. It's not until one tries to approach that 'all' that one can have an inner joy in the face of all sadness and griefs.

You consider then that your mother's influence was more direct than your father's, which might have been perhaps purely musical?

The thing is that when he died I was twelve; so it was an influence without being one, it was a kind of communion. We joked. I wasn't aware of his being a very old gentleman. For me he was someone very gay, with whom one raced down the stairs; a game to see who would arrive at the bottom first. He was a companion. And he would engage in aesthetic discussions, where I had very definite opinions which I'd no longer dare — and which I wouldn't know how — to hold now, but in those days I was absolutely certain. And one day — I'd been running down everything he loved — he said to me, 'Perhaps one day you'll allow that it isn't so bad as that!' And in that 'so bad' was included at the time, I'm ashamed to admit, Verdi himself. I had dreadful prejudices and a conviction that nothing would shift; they were all rooted in my taste for independence.

I remember these discussions, which were quite frequent and which must have entertained him; he must have found this ten-year-old or eleven or nine-year-old, comic — so certain, peremptory, decided and a bit ridiculous — but he loved me!

He remained a musician of his period: he had written many works by then, charming *opéras-comique*, for which there was a taste in France at the time. I have an article here, however, where it says: 'What a pity that M. Boulanger who started out with such talent has become enslaved to the German school and has thus lost his melodic gift.' They had said the same sort of thing about Gounod, and somewhere I have a letter from Gounod to my father: 'Have you been to hear *Faust*? Is it true that the dissonances of the "Prelude" seem intolerable to you?'

One is aware of what took place in people's minds then, something that happens in all periods: a struggle between the past, the present and a future which seems inaccessible but is already the present.

Your father was French, but your mother was Russian?

My father was very French and Mother Russian through and through. When she got married, she thought it necessary to take on everything of my father's; she adopted the French language and immersed herself in his world. Russian was never spoken at home because she did not wish it to be said that a language was spoken in my father's house that he could not understand. I regret that enormously, but I perfectly understand her point of view. She always clung to it. She had a strong personality and a sharp mind, and her judgements usually proved right in the long run.

We sometimes try to trace a clear national influence. Do you think that the Russian element is important to you?

I am sure that it is very important.

But just like my father, I don't like talking about myself, because who would find it interesting? I don't even know to whom I should leave things that I have inherited, because I haven't any family and they don't mean anything to most people. For them, I'm already more in the land of the dead than of the living; so, we can't talk about me all day long because it is of no interest to anyone, especially not to me!

Ernest Boulanger (attributed to Thomas Couture, c.1835),
Nadia Boulanger's father

Juliette Boulanger,
mother of Ernest Boulanger

Princess Michetsky,
wife of Ernest Boulanger

Love at first sight

As a child I couldn't bear the least note of music, I was almost ill, I yelled. I drew crowds. I could not listen to a single note. People could hear my sobs in the street, and they came: 'What is it, Madame? Is your little girl ill?' 'No, she can't bear music.' My father drew thick curtains when giving lessons so as not to disturb his poor miserable crazy child. I had never been near a piano in my life, never. It was a monster that terrified me. And then, one day, suddenly, I discovered it with passion; hearing the fire brigade in the street, I sat down at the piano to try to reproduce the notes. I can still see my father standing there saying, 'What a funny little girl we have!' because he had worried. And from that day on it was music all day long! They couldn't make me leave the piano.

I think in notes before thinking in words, because I didn't learn anything in the normal way. I learnt to read music first, before anything else, and when I was eight — I played music from the time I was three, reading in all the keys, and transposing, I had already worked through part of the treatise on harmony — my mother said to me one day, 'Your eyes are getting a bit better, I think that you would like to read.' And we began to read casually like that, with *Le Général Dourakine*. But I still make mistakes in reading because, without noticing it, I mistake a V for a U; that's how I managed not to fail my driving licence in America because they put me in front of a chart with letters; I said, in one place, V and the poor naïve examiner said 'V?'

'Oh, my mistake, U, I meant to say U . . . H, I mean N . . .'

'Ah,' he said, 'that's better!'

And I got my driving licence not by driving a car, but by reading letters and numbers wrong. My poor eyesight confused them.

Notes speak to me more directly than words. Letters are less familiar to me than notes. When my pupils cannot sight-read some music, I say, 'Oh well, I can't read the paper!' I read the paper more hesitantly than I read a score. Now, if you gave me *Wozzeck* to sight-read, that wouldn't be funny. That's a different kettle of fish. It is a question of difficulty. As though you were to give me a hermetic text, only partly comprehensible. But the connection between letters and their associations is made more slowly in my mind than the association between notes.

What happened? A furious, total passion. I don't much want to talk about all this because it's personal, but the fact is that music is never out of my head, I hear notes, I always hear notes, I am always thinking of notes. It isn't a special skill, it's a fact. I have more difficulty reading a newspaper than a score. Music has become essential to my life along with many other essentials.

Nadia Boulanger, 1894

At home everyone made music; music was the starting point and the centre of our life. My younger sister Lili played music; we were extraordinarily close and attached but quite independent. She roamed about, musically; playing the piano a little, the violin a little, the cello a little, the organ a little, composing. She already had ideas, some of which were to develop in a very moving way. I believe that her whole talent was rooted in her first knowledge of grief. When our father died, she was six years old. And at six she

understood what death was; that it is the grief of surviving someone you love. She never forgot that up to her own death; she
never forgot any detail of our father's life, of his habits, where he
used to put things; the trivial as well as the important things. She
was so gifted that, when still a baby, at two and a half, she used to
sing all the time. Much later, Fauré would come quite often to accom-
pany her; he seemed to be glad to do that because she could sight-
read songs of which she should not normally have understood
anything, yet of which she intuitively seemed to understand everything. As for our education, it was Mother who took things in
hand from the start; when I was seven and she judged that I was
ready to begin harmony, she was incredibly determined — it
made an indelible impression on me — and with me learnt the
entire treatise on harmony by heart. She had never studied
harmony and she learnt it all off by heart, saying to me, 'You have
to reply correctly because it is a subject I know nothing about.'

I loved my teachers. I had exquisite, unforgettable relations
with them but my judge, my witness was always my mother,
because she had the courage to see what I was and what I was
not. We were so deeply attached. She watched everything. She
came to my lessons and at each lesson she always noted everything.

My father died in the previous flat. In our sorrow we kept his
room locked, and looked for somewhere else to live.

We had a lot of trouble with housing because I was a minor, I
could not enter into a lease, and the owners of the buildings
where we tried to rent were nervous of an agreement under
which they would have to accept an organ. They imagined that
the organ would destroy their building and put the neighbours to
flight. So it was very difficult. We looked for months. And then in
October 1904 we came here, to the rue Ballu, where I have been
ever since, and where I began to teach.

The great privilege of teaching consists in getting the students
to really look at what they think, to say what they really want to
say, and to understand clearly what they hear. For this it is
absolutely essential to have a good grounding in language. I did
neither Latin nor Greek, and I'm very often aware of the gap that
this has left. In music I have my limitations, I'm aware of all that I
don't know, but I'm sure of a solid ground because I've been led,
I've been helped and trained to really understand, to listen
properly. And I think that here again my mother's influence has
predominated, because she didn't allow me to do anything without paying proper attention.

The drawing room, rue Ballu

She has been dead a long time, but when I think of her, she is present to me, I sense her. No, I don't have a vision, you understand, it's not that, it isn't superstition. She is with me, she is me, I am her. Time has not touched that. My father died in 1900, that's a long time ago. I was a little girl, but I see him. As I talk to you, he is with us. He is not in the past. If we bring the past with us, it remains present and clarifies the present. If we forget, we have nothing. Everything is obliterated.

Works and Days

Nadia Boulanger entered the Conservatoire very young; she took courses from, among others, Paul Vidal in accompaniment, Louis Vierne and Alexandre Guilmant for the organ, Charles Marie Widor and Gabriel Fauré in composition.

At the Conservatoire, in all the classes that I attended, I was lucky to have astonishing classmates. They were noticeably older than I and there were people such as Jean Gallon who was a marvellous musician, or Georges Enesco. But above all I was in Fauré's class. Fauré had a very great influence on us, clarifying and directing our lives, giving us a sense of dignity, a vision so modest, so tranquil, so detached from life. I can't describe them, but I know these were unforgettable years. All those years I spent in Fauré's class, he never talked about himself, or played a note of his own music. He often had a dreamy air, as if he were somewhere else; we adored him but we sometimes said to each other: 'Today he's not really listening!' The years went by. One day, much later, I went to visit him in the rue des Vignes; he was already ill, already very old, when suddenly in the midst of our conversation he said: 'I'm not sure you did the right thing in giving up composition.'

'Oh,' I replied, '*Cher Maître*, if there's one thing I'm sure of, it is just that. I wrote useless music. I am tough enough with others, so I should be tough with myself.'

He got up, went to the piano and played me part of an exercise that I had written for the class when I was fourteen or fifteen, with a variation perhaps slightly less uninspired than the others. .

With Gabriel Fauré

'Still, there was something in that,' he said.

I embraced him, saying, 'What! You took the trouble . . . and you know it by heart!'

For that day we had thought, 'Today he is not really with us.' In fact, he heard everything, he remembered everything.

I had a surprise when I found myself in Fauré's class and discovered Ravel was there too, doing, as I used to do then, traditional counterpoint. I was insignificant, and did counterpoint, I didn't always find it interesting, yet it seemed quite natural that Ravel should do it. I did it, he did it, we did it. . . . It was only years later that I realized that he had already written his string quartet, and I asked him why he was still studying counterpoint.

'One must clean the house from time to time; I often do it that way,' he replied.

How do you explain that, in contrast to Ravel, Fauré has always been controversial outside France?

I think it's very simple. He is generally unknown. Is Racine popular in Afghanistan?

Well, Racine spoke French and wrote in French.

But so did Fauré. Can you imagine Mozart as a Norwegian? Don't you sense that Stravinsky is Russian? I remember a very nice article by Alfredo Casella saying that there are two ways of being national: by thought or by costume. With Fauré, it is by thought — thought so profound and passionate on the one hand, so detached and chaste on the other. It reminds me of Socrates saying, '. . . and now we part from each other, you to live, I to die. And I wonder who has the better part.'

Mother had her 'days', when she received personal friends on Wednesdays after five. She had some intimate friends, and she lived with people she greatly loved, but she wished the house to be a home for us after my father's death. So on Wednesdays at five, Mother was there.

After I left the Conservatoire in 1904, I began a class and decided 'It will be on Wednesdays.' So Wednesday it was as it still is, after all these years, Wednesday at three o'clock. After the class, Mother received my pupils — life was easier then — she offered them tea, good pastries. She was very generous, she wasn't a greedy person, but took tea like the good Russian she was. So, I've always kept Wednesdays. I am in the same flat and I retain the impression of receiving *chez Maman*.

In my view having a group class is important in more than one respect. Not to see pupils separately is a fatal error, but on the other hand, to give them the sense of thinking or arguing in a group, of knowing what others think, is humanly, if not musically, very necessary. To meet people often, to exchange ideas, to communicate without loss of individuality.

If you have someone in a class who is markedly better than the others, the tendency will be either to pit yourself against him or to be unconditionally devoted: and both reactions are wrong. But sometimes an individual, whether you like it or not, imposes

himself. It was very striking when Saint-John Perse used to come
here. He didn't have any intention of overwhelming anyone, but
very quickly his conversation would become something of a
monologue in front of fascinated listeners. It is the same thing in
class, the best rises to the top. Because he has either a trained or
an intuitive memory, he just has to hear a thing once to retain it.
It's a question of talent.

Do we behave as if this gift of learning, of retention, is a great
favour granted to us, or do we let the days pass through like a
sieve in which nothing remains? And is the residue in this sieve
really an acquisition or just running water? Running water is
water lost.

Fontainebleau

One day at the end of the First World War, General Pershing sent the great conductor Walter Damrosch to Paris, to investigate the state of music in the American army. Damrosch organized a concert; the programme included the Symphony by Saint–Saëns, and he asked me to play the organ part.

It was on that day that a deep friendship was established between us. Damrosch had founded the very first children's concerts. He had set up one thing after another, event after event, concert after concert; he was always inventing something. And one day he said to me: 'What are you doing this summer?'

'I'm going to the country with my family, as usual.'

'Ah, I'm very sorry, but not this summer!'

'Why not this summer? I go every year!'

'I'm very sorry, you will be at Fontainebleau.'

'Heavens, what would I do at Fontainebleau?'

'Well, you come and find out.'

So, I arrived at Fontainebleau to teach classes in English, knowing only 'hello' and 'goodbye' for certain, in fact not understanding a word my pupils said. Among them was Copland, who with Melville Smith was my first American student. General Pershing, knowing that the standard of American music in the army in Europe could be developed and improved, had asked Damrosch to found a school; Francis Casadesus, one of the innumerable Casadesus family, had created a conservatory at Chaumont, under the auspices of the then *sous-préfet*, Monsieur Fragneau. At this juncture, the war ended. Monsieur Fragneau was appointed *préfet* at Melun, and Damrosch declared, 'We mustn't let this slip: we are going to open a school!' What school? Where? How? Why? He was the kind of man who got everything he wanted. Thus with American patronage, with some French support, the American Conservatoire of Fontainebleau was founded in 1921. And thus I got involved. After Francis Casadesus, there were several other directors: Ravel for a while, then Widor, I myself succeeded Robert Casadesus in 1946.

We were very poor, like people who have splendid possessions but nothing to eat. We gave concerts and artists came to them for the pleasure of doing me a favour. The programmes were rather constrained by the fact that they depended on what artists who kindly participated wanted to play. If I had said to them, 'You've never worked on the sonata for solo violin by Bartok? Well, I'd like that in the programme,' they would have sent me packing.

So there were works one could not present. If someone came along proposing that you conduct Stravinsky's *Threni* next week, I hope you would have the good sense to decline the offer!

Besides the concerts, there are — because that is the real purpose of Fontainebleau — master classes. Students keep pouring in to pursue courses in singing, piano, violin, cello, organ, choral singing, conducting and so on. In composition too, of course. All branches of theory. And all these people spend an exhausting, unbearable and delightful summer, from the first of July until the first of September, a summer during which I barely have time for Mass on Sundays.

With the American conductor, Walter Damrosch

I can understand the idea on which the 'Conservatoire Américain de Fontainebleau', was based, after the First World War. The American troops were there, and so it was intended to maintain a certain level of music among them. But why after they left?

I think the Fontainebleau school is very important for the Americans. Because they are brilliant students, very talented people, but the grounding isn't secure in many cases, their ear isn't developed: the basics haven't been drummed into them. Why? Because children mustn't be tired! I believe myself that children who are intelligently tired gain ten years in their studies. The truth is that a class in solfeggio makes you aware that to be a good musician, you must be a good grammarian.

One day I heard a linguist say: 'I allow people to write as they wish, in the style they wish, on the condition that two elements are safeguarded: the horizontal continuity which sustains the vowels and the structure which carries the consonants.' Well, it's exactly that. A student who hasn't been thoroughly trained in this way hears musical surface, but doesn't hear the intermediary lines independently.

I had to insist on a knowledge of essentials. In other words, how to listen, look, hear and see. And then, on having the kind of self-respect which is not assertive, but does attach importance to being. And I believe that if you do not value existence, you cannot play well, you cannot think well, you cannot live well.

You taught them an artistic ethic?

That's a grand word. I used verbs in the infinitive: 'to look, to listen, to hear,' because I can listen and hear nothing, look and see nothing, and above all do something and not like what I am doing — in which case, I disown myself.

In summer I live at Fontainebleau. There is a variety of trees in the English garden which my flat overlooks, in the wing of the château allotted to us for the Conservatoire. It is marvellous. They are all different trees. I don't think I could name one of them. I still don't know the names of trees I've looked at since 1921, because I haven't been sufficiently curious, my will has lacked direction. Deep down I'm ashamed, I am unhappy at not knowing them. I've not been on the lookout.

If only you knew how this matter worries me! All knowledge must be a response to curiosity: in the language of music as in everything else, there are rules. If we succeed in expressing what we want, we can say it in one tongue and translate it. Certain authors lose out, others gain — like Edgar Allan Poe, who was lucky enough to be translated by Baudelaire and Mallarmé; they penetrated the secret of his thought. After hearing only the surface line of a score, a born musician — helped by a knowledge of the essentials — perceives the polyphony of that writing. He sees there are four people in a score, each with different but equal parts; it's no longer a dialogue but a conversation. It is an exchange between all parties.

Drunk on Music

I consume music in an absolutely crazy way. It's like a disease. When I am dead tired, having given eight or nine hours of lessons in succession, the first thing I do — and it irritates everyone in the house — is to turn on the radio! and I listen. I am insatiable. I love to hear. When I was younger, and my sight allowed it, it was just the same, I sight-read all the time.

Rumour has it that you already had an encyclopaedic knowledge of music when you began to teach.

You know, people say a lot of things, very little of which is true. Very well then, let's go into the legend! I have a pupil who is convinced that I finish lessons towards midnight or one o'clock and start again at four. I have never given a lesson at four a.m. I tried to explain that to him and he said, 'I know: I know better!' If so, he knows better than me.

It is true that in winter I did give some lessons at midnight because it was the only time when the Harvard chapel was available; it is true that I said to a man who was determined to have a lesson, although I didn't have the time: 'Tell him, if he is so determined, that I can see him either at midnight or at seven in the morning!'

'Mademoiselle Boulanger takes me for an amateur, she's making fun of me!' I was making a great sacrifice, but he believed I was taking him for a ride and fortunately didn't turn up. I often began my lessons at eight, rarely at seven. Of course at my present age I've had to cut back.

The other evening, I got to the end of the day, I'd begun lessons at eleven o'clock and then without stopping I had reached — with difficulty — about seven o'clock. At that point I said to my student, whom I like very much and who is a very good pianist: 'My dear, I'm done, I must go and lie down.' I had forgotten that another student, young Sermet, a magnificent Turkish pianist was waiting to be introduced. So I asked somebody to tell him that I hadn't an ounce of strength left, that I couldn't meet him. And then, changing my mind, I said to myself, 'That's not fair, let him come to my bedroom.' Never had a pupil entered my bedroom — 'Have him come in.'

Imagine the scene: an old wreck collapsed on a bed in a room, with a gentleman at the piano. It was conducted entirely by the exchange of glances. I think I finally spent two hours with him, and he made great progress during those two hours. And I was bound to enjoy myself: once I was lying down, I was fine. But I worked to the limit of my strength.

Could I have worked even harder? Of course! Why haven't I done so? Because I have let occasions slip. Think of the foolish virgins and the wise virgins, and Valéry saying: 'He who wishes to record his dream has to be awake.'

Legend then is not so far from reality!

And another legend, that I am a neglected genius! . . . Crazy, because the music I have written is useless, not even badly done, useless! It is very offensive. One does not wish to write useless music.

It's you who have deicded that.

Oh, everyone knows!

Has it been played?

Never! Not since I was twenty. But I didn't have to set the whole place on fire to burn everything I had written. I probably kept what was neatly written; happily, I never look at it. If I did, it would be a lesson in humility, a lesson in reason. I would say to myself: 'That's it. From a technical point of view, it is good, it is decent, it has a right to be performed, it is not even an insult to good taste!' It's worse than that.

I don't have to tell you that I dislike hearing *Paillasse*, I don't like it, that's all! But I recognize that the man who wrote it, felt it. He felt it and it doesn't matter that it doesn't suit my taste.

Do you remember that poem by Apollinaire, 'If we were old professors in the provinces, we would not say *ciné*, we would not say *cinéma*, we would say *ci-né-ma-to-graphe*. Therefore, *Mon Dieu*, one must have taste!' In a little aside, just in passing, Apollinaire said something extraordinarily serious, profound. 'Therefore, *Mon Dieu*, one must have taste!' He deals there with a problem that Schopenhauer would have taken eight hundred pages to discuss, and it would be superb, but in a very different form.

Well, the composer who wrote *Paillasse* wrote what he could write and I suppose you understand all the limitations that involves, but he did construct a personal work. My own *oeuvre*, if you can call it an *oeuvre*, is better; it is miles better and miles emptier, because there is nothing to it. There is no personality. If I play the first two notes, G,C, of the quartet in C minor by Fauré, I know at once it is Fauré's, there is a distinctive signature in the ordering of those two notes, which I would find in the same way immediately in Monteverdi or Guillaume de Machaut.

When I decided to abandon composition, it was because I knew that I would never be a great genius. My music could perhaps haved been played, but music played because it is by a good friend doesn't interest me at all.

Still, there is a lot of music which is perfectly respectable, without being imperishable masterpieces.

There is! There must be! It provides a 'mattress' for the great masterpieces. There must be a mattress for them to lie on.

You know how to appreciate good or bad construction in a work, but what in your opinion is the criterion for a masterpiece?

I don't know; I won't say that it does not exist, but I don't know what it is.

And yet, faced with a masterpiece, you feel quite certain.

For me, this always comes back to faith. As I accept God, I accept beauty, I accept emotion. I also accept masterpieces.

I believe that there are conditions without which masterpieces cannot be achieved, but I also believe that what defines a masterpiece cannot be pinned down.

Then you apply an unknown criterion to your own music.

No. I simply say: 'To be or not to be! That is the question!'

And then there's Tintoretto's aphorism: 'Good colours aren't bought on the Rialto!' I simply couldn't buy genius.

The Cardinal Virtues

Attentiveness

I have been to Athens only once, for three hours. That changed my life forever. I saw the Acropolis, I saw what made us what we are, the source of all that is precious, profound and joyous in us. 'It is because passion is alive that the Greeks made a goddess of Minerva,' wrote Maurras. As a child, I dreamt of Greece, and the very word 'Greece' aroused in me more than I could express or even know.

I had the good fortune to be brought up by a remarkably intelligent mother. She adored me — she had lost a child before I was born, so I was a miraculous new arrival — but she loved me enough to be dispassionate in her judgements. There was one thing she could not tolerate: lack of attention. From the first I grew up with this absolute attentiveness, which is vital to self-awareness. People often seem to lack it now, yet it's essentially a form of character. With certain people there is such a force of concentration that everything becomes important; with others, everything passes and is forgotten, they repeat their actions from day to day. No evolution is possible because whatever is produced immediately dissolves. And then there are people who take twenty, forty, fifty years to find what they are looking for.

So before encouraging anyone, you must find out whether they're capable of loving, of interesting themselves in what they're doing, whatever it may be, for its own sake. This is a fundamental distinction between people, it makes some extraordinarily active, and others what I call sleepers. Let the sleepers lie — there is no point in waking them up. They are nice, happy, polite; unobjectionable as people; they are what they are.

I don't know whether attentiveness can be taught. I would say

that anyone who acts without paying attention to what he is
doing is wasting his life. I'd go as far as to say that life is denied by
lack of attention, whether it be to cleaning windows or trying to
write a masterpiece. It takes us back to that marvellous page of
Bergson, where he explains that man is confronted with the
chaos of nature, and that, to a certain degree, it is given him to
organize it. In these conditions, man found he was capable of
much more thought, of much more understanding, than he had
believed possible: 'Philosophers who speculate on this question
have not sufficiently stressed that when the desired end is
reached, nature gives a sign.' Bergson adds this marvellous
image: 'This sign is joy; I can only define it as the divine essence.'
And he concludes waspishly: 'One looks for praise in the exact
proportion that one is unsure of success. He who is sure does
not seek any approval, he knows.' So what is it, this force which
makes saints, heroes, geniuses, which makes men pursue their
destinies to the end? It is given to everyone. It applies as much to
Wagner writing his *Ring* cycle as to the anonymous window-
cleaner, or to the baby that we believe has only a rudimentary
form of consciousness. I don't know whether you like babies,
you're probably too young; I love them, but they make me
anxious, because I don't know how to cope with them. But I'll
never forget the day I took a child of fourteen months a parcel
with a little bear or something of the sort. He wasn't at all
interested in the toy. He was fascinated by the string! You could
not have distracted his mind and his little fingers from undoing
the knot.

There are people who shake hands like a dead fish — not very
pleasant. Conversely, when some people shake your hand you
register an exchange, however brief, an extraordinary exchange
between that person and you. And both will soon die, disappear,
or rather, assume an unknown form.

There is a phrase in *Hamlet,* which I think of absolutely every
day of my life, without exception: 'Words without thoughts
never to Heaven go.' If I say 'Good Morning' to you without
thinking, I don't exist. When we were in Rome, my sister was
nineteen, she'd won the Prix de Rome, she was there in all her
grace, all her guilelessness. We were walking in the gardens of
the Villa Medici. In the gardens, we had the illusion of youth
which thinks it will last forever, and there was also an old woman
doing the weeding, her skin all wrinkled, with traces of what
must have been extraordinary beauty. This was in 1913, and it
still plays a very important part in my life. We passed, she raised

her head, she smiled an ineffable smile and said to us: *'Buon giorno, e per tutto il giorno.'* The smile by itself was a gift. We must have understood, and thanked her. Sixty-five years have gone by, my sister died in 1918, but when I hear that phrase, I say to myself: 'Never forget that your days are blessed. You may know how to profit by them or you may not, but they are blessed.'

Do you think that it is intolerable, too serious an attitude to life? I don't mind if it seems intolerable, ridiculous or naïve; I owe my greatest joys — as I imagine other people do — to those moments when I've seized what was given and experienced it not superficially but profoundly.

Nadia and Lili Boulanger

That overwhelming moment produced by the *'Buon giorno, e per tutto il giorno'* was nothing in itself, it was only an old woman gathering old weeds, but she had a crystalline soul. It gave her a kind of genius of the heart, a sanctity of spirit, and having nothing to express but what her heart inspired, she created something beyond herself, beyond me. She perceived the existence of something which made the day fine, she knew it was beautiful and everything deriving from it was a means of grace.

It seems to me that attention is the state of mind which allows us to perceive what has to be. It is a form of the vision experienced by the great mystics, on days when they were granted a profound concentration. Saint Teresa of Avila often comes to my mind. Great saint that she was, great spirit that she was, she still had what she called 'days of dry prayer', when she prayed and prayed — she never ceased to pray — but there was nothing! And then a day would come when she would hear. In art we call this inspiration. It is the moment when a man succeeds in grasping his thought, his real thought, right at the core; the moment when we touch the truth, when communion is established. This year there was a concert by Menuhin, an altogether superb concert. He gave a number of encores and the last was the slow movement of Brahms's sonata in D minor. What happened then was part of an indescribable completeness: the whole house found itself in the grip of the same mute emotion, which created silence of an extraordinary quality. Everyone understood, felt, participated in what he himself must have been feeling. I don't think he will ever forget that moment. In some way it passed beyond him, to a higher level, which we very rarely reach. We are too weak to scale those heights very often, to realize the potential available if we could really commune with ourselves.

Another example. I remember recently attending Rostropovitch's rehearsals for *Tosca*. Rightly or wrongly, I could survive quite well without listening to *Tosca*, which I recognize is a masterpiece, but I can live without it. Yet I know I shall never forget those rehearsals. He came to see me at the end of one, and said in his slightly broken French: 'When I undertake something, it must be done as well as possible.' For him each note is essential. He can't stand a single indifferent note, and though many would have been satisfied with the first results, he repeated some passages an extraordinary number of times with such good humour, with such an incapacity to be impatient, that the orchestra, charmed by rehearsing, was euphoric. Each musician gave of his best in the euphoria created by the absolutely dis-

interested determination of Rostropovitch. He wanted the music
to reach its best level. And he succeeded because he is such a
great artist!

But each to his own highest level. Everyone should try to
stretch himself; otherwise the great would remain isolated
behind a barrier.

If you talk to André Malraux, for example, your attention is
stretched — his thoughts are so quick, sometimes he doesn't
finish a sentence — that in order to follow him, you have to
develop a new sort of attention yourself.

I have the impression that the more I try to think of the
essentials of music, the more they seem to depend on general
human values. It's all very well to be a musician, it's all very well
to be a genius, but the intrinsic value which constitutes your
mind, your heart, your sensibility, depends on what you are. You
may have to lead a life in which no one understands who you are.
Nevertheless I believe that everything depends on attention. I
only see you if I pay attention. I only exist, in my own eyes, if I
pay attention to myself.

One always comes back, willy nilly, to the great words. Have
you or have you not received grace? Saint Teresa of Avila,
afflicted despite everything with arid prayer, has visions; we say
to ourselves, 'She is mad, it is hysteria.' That's very convenient!
Was Menuhin hysterical while playing sublimely a sublime
movement of a Brahms sonata? No, he received the power to
penetrate a thought which is neither Brahms's nor his, nor mine;
a thought floating in the world, above the world, bearing light.

Desire

When you have the opportunity, as I do, to deal with people
just setting out — most of them are twenty, some eighteen,
others thirty, it doesn't matter — you suddenly discover in some
of them such a longing for life that you know they will do
whatever they do with love, with a feeling of abundance which
comes from desire. Everything is there. Are we capable of desire,
a permanent sense of discovery?

One day I was invited by Turks to hear *Oedipus* in Turkish, admirably done. I knew *Oedipus* by heart, as we all do, so their speaking in Turkish didn't bother me at all. I followed the thought. If I hadn't known my Sophocles, I would never have guessed that Oedipus was Jocasta's son and that he had killed his father, never . . . not the slightest suspicion. It's something that wouldn't enter your head.

Although you know how the play unfolds, it develops in such a way that the moment comes when you are taken by surprise. I find that miraculous, I thank God and bow before the miracle. You can talk to great actors: each time they take up some piece they have played all their lives, it is a rediscovery. That is the privilege of emotion: if I know how to look at you, you surprise me each time. If I accustom myself to seeing you, without grasping that each time can offer a different insight, you become a piece of furniture I don't think about any longer, and the loss is mine.

That you should be here, that you should be who you are, I find that a profound mystery. And if it isn't a profound mystery, you are a nuisance to me. Because I've no desire merely to see you.

Mother used to say to us: 'Ah, please don't start hugging me at the same time every night, it'll become a habit.' When I was a little girl I was sight-reading — in what must have been a scandalous way — the last sonatas of Beethoven (can you imagine!), it seemed to me that I was playing them better than anyone else could. I changed my opinion afterwards, but I still hear those works as if for the first time.

I wouldn't like to say to myself: 'I like so and so a lot, but less than I used to.'

That has never happened in my life. I have never abandoned any friendship. It seems to me that the sign of old age, the real sign — and I have all of them except this — would be not to attach importance to things. I think of this often in my regret at not speaking Russian, because that Russian heritage speaks strongly in me. I regret not knowing and not speaking Russian, or Latin either, which inevitably cuts me off from my roots; and I'm ashamed to have to admit that if I'd had courage and resolved to learn one word a week for ten years — that's not a lot, one word a week — I could have read all of Russian literature. Now, have I read it? No. I have to search for the letters to read my own name in Russian. It's the result of my negligence, of my indifference. I only had to learn it. No one prevented me and nothing stopped me from learning one word a week. If my desire is such that my natural laziness prevents me realizing it, then the desire isn't very strong.

Recently, someone carried out an odd project: to count how many notes Schubert wrote. Perhaps his energy was somewhat misplaced. He arrived at a horrifying number and asked the following question: 'Leaving aside genius, how much time would it take simply to write this number of notes?' After investigating the matter, he found that it would take about twenty-five years. Well, Schubert only took fifteen years to put millions of notes on paper. Where did this power come from? Schubert didn't say to himself 'I should like to speak Russian.' He did it instead of talking about it. We talk about what we don't do, and the great excuse we offer is lack of time. But Schubert didn't have time, Bach didn't have time, Fauré didn't have time, no one has time! They found time — that's why Plato is still alive to us today. That is why you must say to children every day: 'It depends on you, o passer-by, whether I am tomb or treasury. It depends on you, friend; do not enter without desire.' Those words of Valéry's are inscribed on the walls of the Trocadero.

I knew Valéry well, but I knew Stravinsky even better. Stravinsky was a great believer and in his art you sense the sacred. The day this man, who always accepted commissions, decided to write a mass, as he had decided, years before, to write 'Ave Maria', the 'Lord's Prayer' and the 'Credo', he was responding with a ritual gesture to his faith — the faith which determined that if he played cards, he would play seriously and as well as he could. In all his actions there was something serious, even amidst frivolity or burlesque. Think of the 'Circus Polka', for example. He was so happy when he was asked to write 'Circus Polka' for the elephant act in a circus. When I went to California to see him, he'd just finished writing it, and he told me to go and hear it performed in New York, and tell him about it afterwards. He was euphoric at having succeeded in writing 'Circus Polka'. Many people have insinuated that he was ready to do anything for money. But he would himself have paid to write this 'Circus Polka'. It had so entertained him. But there is no confusing 'Circus Polka' and the *Symphony of Psalms;* no mock religion, no stagey signs of the cross!

I asked him one day, 'Are you going to accept such and such a commission?' He replied with this marvellously elliptic phrase: 'I can't, it doesn't make my mouth water.' Valéry said, 'Do not enter without desire' and Stravinsky said, 'that doesn't make my mouth water.'

That goes for great as well as little things. I don't think that in itself, playing cards is criminal, and so if it amuses me to play patience, I at least want to do it properly. Moving a card from left to right and right to left, is either stupid or very important, even in its uselessness. It is useless to write a masterpiece, it is useless to think.

That a fine fellow called Johann Sebastian Bach wrote the *St John Passion*, the *St Matthew Passion*, is unknown to most people, or else they couldn't care less, and take not the least joy in them. But what do you think it takes for this immensely important event to survive?

It seems to me that Johann Sebastian Bach is the vital element.

Well, not to me; *you* are, because the *St Matthew Passion* doesn't exist if you do not listen to it. When I had read a new book by Valéry, I would say to him, 'What a marvel, what an incredible achievement!' And Valéry would reply: 'But it is you who have made it.' You'd be surprised for a moment.

I don't know whether, when you were little, you were as struck as I was by the Evangelist's saying, 'For whosoever hath, to him shall be given.' I was incensed. 'What, he has already received a lot and he will be given even more!' However, there is great wisdom in that because what good does it do to give a lot to someone who has nothing and will do nothing because he has no desire in him?

One day a pupil of mine went for a piano lesson with a very well-known teacher, who greeted him with, 'It's terrible, you know, to be a talented artist and to be reduced to giving lessons.' My pupil, bad-mannered but really inspired, said: 'Well, Monsieur, if you are wasting time giving lessons, you won't waste it with me, because I'm going.' And he left. I told him: 'You are very bad-mannered, but you've done the right thing in telling him that, because no one is obliged to give lessons. It poisons your life if you give lessons and it bores you.'

Are you interested by your pupils' personalities to varying degrees?

Yes, but it's also interesting to find out why one doesn't interest you. That's sufficient. If you're interested by nature, everything interests you.

Obviously, if by a certain time I see that a pupil hasn't any talent, I will say: 'Listen, I think you're wrong to carry on with a course which isn't for you.' But someone who hasn't much of an ear, who doesn't know much and who takes the trouble to learn, to develop what he knows without having particular talent, can be of great service to somebody eventually, by showing that to learn a skill is already a victory, already progress, the satisfaction of an inner desire. It is easier to reject effort than to appreciate it.

I had a Polish student whose father had shut the piano and only permitted his academic studies, which were brilliant. At twenty-one, he still had not touched a piano, but he decided, 'Whatever Papa thinks, I want to be a musician, I want to be . . . a pianist.' He sought out the Director of the Warsaw Conservatory, Monsieur Sikorsky, and said:

'Monsieur, I've come to ask you for piano lessons.'

'Well, play me something.'

'The thing is, I can't play.'

'And why do you want lessons?'

'I want to become a pianist, I want to play the great concertos.'

'But my boy, you can't, you are twenty-one, you know nothing about music, it's impossible. I haven't the right to encourage you. Better to give up, believe me.'

He went away, saying to himself, 'I've been talking to an honest man, but I'm determined to become a pianist.' He began work on his own. After six months, he wrote to Sikorsky: 'Monsieur, I realize I am being indiscreet, but my whole life depends on your decision and judgement. I think I've made some progress. Would you give me ten minutes of your time? Would you hear me play?' Sikorsky invited him along. He had made such progress that Sikorsky was moved to tears. He gave him lessons every day; at thirty-one, Wojtowicz was playing the great concertos, the whole repertoire, and he became a teacher at the Warsaw Conservatory. It is an incredible story. He is still alive, I see him whenever I go to Poland. He found the way to become a great pianist.

I believe there was someone in Bergson's circle, his right-hand man in a way, who at thirty-five declared, 'I'm really very drawn to Chinese.' Bergson said to him: 'My dear chap, you cannot begin Chinese at your age. To be able to do anything decent in Chinese, you have to learn to transcribe thousands of signs. You can't do it.'

'Yes, I know, I know, but there are summons one simply has to obey.'

And he succeeded.

After all, Rameau wrote his first opera at fifty. And you have the example, the miracle of Roussel, a naval officer who graduated from the Naval Academy, without professional access to music until he was twenty-five. Those who teach phonetics say that until a child is eight years old it has no accent in a foreign language. Of course, you feel there are moments when Roussel is self-conscious. You never feel that Mozart or Haydn is self-conscious. You never feel Schubert is awkward.

To think that a man with everything against him can overcome all obstacles by courage, will, energy, vital powers! I find that more impressive than the result itself; it's a joy to see that all effort bears fruit. And then, you must take the time to savour. To eat is to taste. Stravinsky used to taste. He didn't eat fast. He savoured. I almost never taste. I eat a meal while giving a lesson and I don't notice what I eat. And then suddenly there's something extraordinary, a peach . . . Two years ago, I had a cherry that was a masterpiece of a cherry. From time to time I think of it. I've never eaten its equal.

Memory

The *Well-Tempered Clavier* has been with me throughout my life. When my father died I already knew it by heart. That must have satisfied him, because I think he had it by heart too.

You were twelve and you knew it by heart?

I had to. Each week I had to play a prelude and fugue by heart. But you know, you mustn't exaggerate, a prelude and fugue a week, that's not much! In my course I require as much of my pupils. I make them write out the separate parts from memory after which they should be able to reconstruct the whole piece. After a training of this kind, they have well-furnished minds. In fact I get the most out of this class, because each note interests me and takes on a new dimension.

But these are draconian demands!

Draconian, savage!

I think it was Montaigne who said: 'Without memory I have no past, I have no present, I have only something fugitive which is linked with nothing.' We are eternally faced with the equation: living in the past, living in the present, living in the future. It is what Bergson points to in his significant remarks on 'Memory, presence, anticipation', or St Thomas Aquinas: 'One must feel the presence of the past, the presence of the present and presence of the future.' Reading or listening to music, if you don't remember the preceding notes and don't sense the notes to come, you're reading isolated characters that make no sense. Music, especially, implies the phenomenon of memory. But the same goes for painting. It's not true or accurate that when I look at a picture, I see everything simultaneously. I say, 'It's a crucifixion' or 'It's an apple on a chair', but I don't see it all. At the moment I see the apple, I don't see the bar of the chair, I don't see the wicker-work on which the dish is placed. I dissociate the images. First, of course, you must perceive the terms, the means, the signs; then see them successively, together, through the intermediary of memory which reconstitutes them.

You remember a most impressive amount of music. It seems that neither accumulation nor age has lessened your musical memory.

I don't think so, but I doubt that I retain the ability to learn new things as quickly, because before I used to see them — not only hear them, but see them. It had already become difficult, but over the last two years, impossible. A written page has become blurred for me. I see that something is written there, but I don't know what. No idea what it is — not a hint! That could have been my death-sentence. Well, I look at it fondly. This nearly total blindness doesn't bother me when it comes to all the music that's been with me for so many years. On the other hand, new manuscripts sent to me by old pupils pose a problem; as I've no idea what's in them, someone deciphers them for me, Narcis Bonet for instance.

At the piano?

Certainly, unless there's a tape.

And a single hearing enables you to perceive everything?

That depends on the works, some require several hearings. When we go to Monaco for the composition contest, Narcis Bonet comes with me. He plays all the instrumental parts one after the other, then a few at a time, or all together; I think that by the end of our jury deliberations I know the scores quite well. But it takes time. There are many things I don't hear because I let them go. If we remembered the hundredth part of what we had read, learnt and loved in our lives, we would be impenetrable riddles to one another.

Thank God, we discard a little of what we know.

Ah! No, no — sadly! I should like to remember everything. Not the useless details; it doesn't worry me that I don't recall the Köchel numbers. I haven't a memory for figures, whether important or trivial. But do I refuse to have that sort of memory, or do I accept not having it? I have learnt much and forgotten much. Georges Enesco, with his prodigious memory, was for me one of those impenetrable riddles. Years after only one hearing of a piece, no matter how vast, he could recite to you the separate parts. Mitropoulos, Casella, they had tremendous memories too.

Today I believe that Messiaen has a very good memory and Boulez an astounding one. He knows everything by heart. If he had to work normally at conducting all he conducts, he would have had to give up a long time ago; the weight of his repertoire would have killed him. As it is, he just sees, then remembers!

In spite of everything, one thing remains of my visual memory: I know where to look for the piece I need in a score. I'm usually right. Otherwise I wouldn't guess at it. Usually when I'm sure, I insist, saying: 'Listen, I tell you it's on the right-hand page, perhaps it's not among the waltzes, perhaps it's not in that volume, but it is on the right.' And it does turn up on the right. The waltz I adore is at the bottom of the page, on the right. I know it's there, wedged in, there's scarcely room for it to breathe, but it's there!

You have music everywhere in your flat. Your considerable library continues to expand. Is there room for more?

It's dreadful, I don't know what to do. I haven't an heir, it's a catastrophe.

I still have my grandmother's library. She won prizes at the Conservatoire in 1812, and I have them here. I have all my father's manuscripts; he was a very respectable musician, not a genius, but a very good musician. I have all his scores, I have two great shelves full of orchestral scores from my grandmother. And then I have all the library that has accumulated and which expands by the week.

My paternal grandmother was a very famous singer. She sang in my father's first opera, and her library contained scores of Mozart, Gluck, Boïeldieu, Auber, all of her repertoire. This was in another era; she had been dead a long time when I was born. My father adored her and I preserve everything. You understand, I wouldn't for the world sell my grandmother's scores; I would prefer to give them away, without knowing to whom, when I take my one-way ticket. I have read them often. As a child, I learnt to read the orchestra in these scores.

There are pocket scores which would seem easier to use?

There's no question of that; one can't take the place of the other. One is a score that has been in my father's and his mother's hands. I can't compare it with a score I could buy.

Your musical library continues to grow?

Every day.

You receive manuscripts?

Every day. Well, every day is a slight exaggeration, but I'm sure that on an average I get at least five a week.

But what do you do with them?

I keep them, because I don't throw things away easily. There's something conceited in the act of discarding. It's contemptuous, it offends me. After all, who am I to decide that such and such a work is not good enough for me to keep? But what we're talking about only represents a tiny part of my library.

I have the *Bachgesellschaft* [the complete edition of Bach's works], the complete Mozart, Purcell, Monteverdi — complete in two editions — Palestrina, Orlando di Lasso, Dufay — in so far as his is complete. I was lucky enough to be given the *Bachgesellschaft* when I was twelve, because a friend said to my godmother who used to send me extravagant presents: 'Listen, I'm sure we're being silly in giving her just anything, she'll surely be a musician; let's give her the *Bachgesellschaft* over two or three years.' And thus I acquired my *Bachgesellschaft*.

And once you had the Bachgesellschaft, *Mozart followed?*

No, Mozart I bought some years ago. I buy scores here and there.

Don't you think that there are bound to be pieces that aren't of any value in these sets?

Oh, not that many; I haven't a critical mind when I read music, I take pleasure in encountering it. I read or have read to me at least once, without delay, all the manuscripts I receive. As for Mozart, he can wait. Do you know Lully's marvellous answer when someone said during a rehearsal: 'Hurry up, the King is waiting.'

'The King can wait, he is the master!'

So, Mozart can wait. He is the master!

What is the difference for you between a reading with sound and a purely visual reading?

They are different pleasures, addressed to different senses. You have the help that imagination gives reading, and if it is hard to produce at a piano — like a score by Xenakis for example — you struggle over sight-reading. If you are only reading, you comprehend more easily, you are not bothered by the way your hands can be paralysed. But there are times when you can't imagine unexpected sound effects. I don't think it would be possible to imagine the effect of the crescendo of *Daphnis* without hearing this dazzling, blinding sound. And reading lacks that physical pleasure. The audible is an indispensable complement to the visual.

Bach and Webern have written works that are astounding in terms of counterpoint. It is good to be able to analyse them by reading, but the *Art of Fugue* is nevertheless meant to be heard. All music is made to be heard, even if the composer himself can do without hearing it. Beethoven only achieved his true freedom when he could no longer hear, and he dared to conceive everything he could imagine. It's sad to say, because in human terms it's very cruel; to be deprived of one sense renders the others sharper. But to hear is a grace, to remember is a grace.

I am old, I am bent, I no longer play the piano; but in the meantime I am never alone, I have learnt so much by heart!

Ever since the organ class, I have always had company. Around 1912, Stravinsky joined it; since then, I've seen my pupils' music. There are those whose work I do not like but who interest me with their research (those who search). And then there are those whom I don't like at first and one day I end up understanding.

You must store up a lot of things in the memory, it's a way of having company, good company in oneself. Everything we know by heart enriches us and helps us find ourselves. If it should get in the way of finding ourselves, it is because we have no personality. True personality is complemented by the personalities of others. Father Teilhard de Chardin has explained this eloquently. 'In a couple, one should not be absorbed by the other, each should be influenced by the other's differences.'

Everything that brings us into contact with great minds, minds inspired by noble motives, helps us to rise above the humdrum. If we have learnt a lot by heart, we always have company. And what company! The royal company of the centuries' great masterpieces.

Craftsmanship

Two Attitudes

There are two ways of approaching music: it is quite possible to know nothing while fully sensing melodic emotion, musical emotion. And the music charms you, transports you; above all you must respect this feeling and not spoil it with false efforts at knowledge. You can't work at Greek for three months. It's a waste of energy. Either you *know* that you don't know Greek and despair of it; or you take the necessary time, ten years, fifteen, twenty, thirty years, it doesn't matter. You will never tire of it; you do what you love, that's what you choose to do. It's unbearable on discouraging or boring days, but you do it, because it has become vitally necessary.

Emotion without knowledge is perfectly respectable, though. You can't expect at a stroke to initiate the general public into technical terms. Not everyone can study theology and work on the Church Fathers. It would be pointless.

Obviously there are people who experience nothing when they hear music. I had a medical friend whom music didn't affect a bit. There was no connection between him and music; it didn't bother him, it didn't carry an emotional charge for him. And yet this man was very intelligent, sensitive, refined, perceptive about lots of things, but not about music. Whatever you make of it, that's an exceptional case. On the other hand, I know eminently intelligent people who can say nothing about music. It touches them, it moves them. That's all. They're happy with that sensation, and that's the end of it. But emotion has a regenerating power, and the emotion of a non-specialist audience is essential.

One day during the war, General Huntziger said to me: 'Would you come and play music for my soldiers?'

'Listen,' I said to him, 'I don't do that sort of thing. What I'd suggest wouldn't be the sort of thing they want.'

'You don't understand, they know the situation is very grave. I should like to show them there is something better, to let them hear beautiful things.'

'You are the commanding general here. If you appoint me commander-in-chief of music, I will send you a programme and we'll each take our chances.'

And I worked out a programme, being careful to include pieces that were quite short and eloquent, but all of them masterpieces. I arrived at the hall, in the vicinity of Sedan; there were eight hundred soldiers, and I said to myself, 'This will turn out badly. This programme is too severe, even though the pieces are short — it can't be helped!'

Half way through the concert I had placed 'Dieu, qu'il la fait bon regarder', one of Debussy's *Chansons de Charles d'Orléans*. It's the only time in my life that it's had to be sung three times. It moved them profoundly. After that, General Giraud asked me to go to Saint Omer, this time for an orchestral programme. He had brought together all the soldiers who were at all musical to make a kind of orchestra, and again it was a programme of masterpieces. Everything went off magnificently, they were enchanted; there was nothing but the best.

All the same, I wondered if I'd put some rowdy piece in the middle, whether that would have been the great success . . .

I've been to give concerts in factories two or three times, and I've said to the people there: 'You have a profession I don't know, I have a profession you don't know. I bring you and can give you only what I believe to be the best.' And they couldn't be fooled. They understood perfectly, they were absolutely at one with the music. Would they be able to follow the canons of the *Musical Offering* with the same satisfaction? It would be interesting to try it out because, despite the purely intellectual aspect of these canons, they create an emotion which is music itself, and ignorance can be balanced by an extraordinary intuitive love. Only a few people are born with the ability to comprehend an abstract work.

What I don't really understand is why there's a difference between a masterpiece of purity by Mozart and a bit of successful pop music. I believe it's in the mind, but I'm not too sure. I ask myself: does the man Mozart or the man Bach have an order of thought which takes you into another sphere of emotional activity, sensual activity, technical activity? Is the object different? Am I the same person, listening to a pop-song or attending Mass? I don't reflect much on this matter, because to me it seems a fact. And I can't find a satisfactory explanation for this fact. But everything that goes beyond the everyday level seems to belong to the same sphere.

The ability to enjoy even the least structurally complex music always denotes musical intuition. That needs to be preserved and sustained if possible. The question is, how may such intuition be nurtured?

Awakening Sounds

In most elementary education, the right to learn how to listen, a child's birthright, is seldom taken into account. Children are made to see, they are made to feel a little (not a lot), they are made to choose (very seldom), but not to listen. All children, from the time they're four, know their right from their left hands. They know colours. I don't understand why they shouldn't know sounds, even if they are never to become musicians. They learn words, they learn gestures, signs, and there is one area in which they learn nothing: music. They hear notes without knowing what they represent. The energetic repercussion of a rhythm, of a developing melody, of combinations of sound, can give them great excitement; but knowing about these sounds will take away nothing of the excitement.

Do you think that the power of naming is linked to perception? In other words, that consciousness is a condition of pleasure?

I don't know whether this puzzles you, but I've never declared 'This object is yellow' and had someone else tell me, 'No, it's red, or blue.' And yet if I look at a painting, I discover that the painter has seen shadows and lights that I couldn't even have imagined. Everything depends on the angle and power of perception.

Do you know what Valéry wrote in *Leonardo?* 'We are told that the sea is flat, we do not see that it is standing up in front of us.' It's probably the same thing with sound. It produces phenomena of the same order.

My teacher Louis Vierne was born blind. He had an operation

when he was twenty-six and could see a little. He found one thing unbearable, the way a head is attached to the neck and shoulders. For him, that was horrible. Also, if he was told: 'Pick up this pencil!' he would answer, 'I can't, it's too far away'. But he would want to pick up a house because it was large and he saw it close up. It took him one or two years to understand the relationship of large and small to proximity or distance. He used to see large objects as close and small ones as distant.

But to what degree does any of us see things as they really are? Someone who hears the organ will say, 'Oh!, it must take such strength!' Now, to play an organ with five hundred stops, you exercise the same pressure as when you play a little pipe-organ with two pedals. Those who hear the organ for the first time are stunned by its power. One doesn't employ extra force. One obtains the musical colouring by external means, in much the same way a shadow plays on the colour of an object.

It seems to me that a language can only exist on a large base of conventions solidly established and accepted by those who use it.

Harvard, 1941

When I open a dictionary of scientific words, I blush with shame because I can read a whole page without understanding a word, yet in this void I cannot grasp, there is a world of science. If I am utterly ignorant of music, I react simply: 'This makes a noise, a noise that is more or less agreeable.'

As soon as I develop, I perceive many more things and if I have the ear of a Boulez, I hear a G or some other note with all the harmonic world it carries in itself. I have the power to dissociate them and to reassociate them.

It would be absurd to think that fundamental ignorance helps the hatching of personality. To learn and to know add to the purely intuitive feelings of those who naturally love music.

Recently I received from an old pupil a letter that really struck me: 'When I came to the class, you announced — in quite a disagreeable way, if I may say so — "Either you devote your whole life to music, or you abandon it now!"'

But the essential condition of everything you do, and not only in music, the touchstone, must be choice, love, passion. You do it because you consider that the marvellous adventure of being alive depends entirely on the atmosphere you yourself create, by your enthusiasm, your conviction, your understanding. But without a thorough technique, you cannot even express what you feel most intensely. And it is here that the teacher comes in.

On Teaching

Without limiting yourself to a 'system', surely in your process of analysis you must judge, distinguish, classify the works in question?

I have never pretended to set out a philosophy of music — even less to establish a hierarchy — I'm not in the running for that.

Because you think it's uninteresting?

No, it's simple. I know that Buxtehude's music is very fine, but if you said to me, 'Tell me how, why and how much. . .', I would say, 'Listen. . .'.

You need an established language and then, within that established language, the liberty to be yourself. It's always necessary to be yourself — that is a mark of genius in itself.

All a teacher can do is develop in the pupil the faculties that will permit him to handle his instrument. What he does with it is beyond the teacher's scope. I can't provide anyone with inventiveness, nor can I take it away; I can simply provide the liberty to read, to listen, to see, to understand. But I find there are a lot of musicians who quite simply do not hear things. That doesn't make me doubt; it confirms my view that they haven't had liberty, only license. Ask a violinist to play the bass line of a concerto or a sonata, while humming the violin part, and you will find even very good violinists incapable of doing it. Well then, they must be disciplined.

I knew a little violinist, still a child but already very successful at school, and I said to him one day,

'Sing me the Mendelssohn concerto, the slow movement, sing me . . . the bass!'

'But I don't know it.' He was about twelve years old.

'Well, we'll look for it, do you think it's there?'

After we had reconstructed the bass line, he understood what he rested on. He was no longer suspended over a void. Everyone who has learnt to hear plays in a different way, it's quite obvious.

It's the same with musicians in an orchestra. Given the necessary time, the role of a conductor, essentially, consists in making each musician conscious of the others' parts. I have always enjoyed the greatest co-operation from musicians. It was enough for me to say, for example, to the double basses at the beginning of Fauré's *Requiem*: 'Gentlemen, I am counting on you, it is so important: listen'. They understood straight away and played everything with concentration, I only had to glance at them.

The only thing I can do for my pupils is to put at their fingertips the liberty that knowledge gives of the means of self-expression; it is to lead them by an established process, by an imposed discipline, to retrieve the essentials of language.

I believe that a man is made of all that comes before him. In Mozart's life there was the marvellous presence of his father, so unjustly judged, who gained him so many years by his support and strictness. Loving a child doesn't mean giving in to all his whims; to love him is to bring out the best in him, to teach him to love what is difficult. Leopold Mozart taught his son to overcome the impossible. He didn't ask more than he was capable of, but then his son could do everything.

There is much talk of reforms in teaching. I don't know what ought to be done, but I know that there is something I should like to see enforced. It would be simply asking the question, 'What do you think, my friend?' What is important is that he should indeed think something; whether it's crazy, intelligent, or odd doesn't really matter as long as he can express it properly.

I ask my pupils: you say the word 'modulation', you say 'chord', you say 'fugue', what do these words suggest to you? One day at the École Normale, in a course on the history of music, I announced: 'We are going to study the fugue this year. Who knows what a fugue is?' One hand was raised, by a little girl of fourteen or fifteen:

'The fugue is a polyphonic composition for several voices.'

And do you know any fugues?'

'Oh! No, Mademoiselle, oh no!' As though I had accused her of something scandalous! She was repeating it like a parrot. There are those who answer, even wrongly, because they've thought of something, and others who stammer, who try to guess what I want. I have a student who is very nice, but frightened. He wants to please me, he wants me to like his harmony. He plays and then turns towards me, desparately anxious:

'Is that just how it should be?'

I say, 'But I've no idea, I don't know what you want. As long as I don't know what you want, musically you don't exist for me.'

What do you look for in a pupil? Is it artistic resolve first of all?

Choice, artistic determination, taste. My role is above all to try to understand what he is and not what I am. When a pupil repeats what I've said, I retort:

'Listen, that's not important. What do you think of it yourself? Say it awkwardly, say what you like and if you can't think of anything to say, say so and then learn your rules.' That's another province, that's the machinery; the rules must be learnt by heart, like the multiplication table, because it's complicated to have to begin from the beginning when your multiplication or division goes wrong.

When you accept a new pupil, the first thing is to try to understand what natural gift, what intuitive talent he has. Often enough you'll discover this very easily, if you really respect children. It's a serious question: can you go ahead and develop a child in quite a different direction from his parents, without being absolutely certain that his is a talent that should be developed and stimulated? I have a student who has made fantastic progress . . . in twenty-five years. Twenty-five years is a long time! But today she's able to teach in a little American town, teaching the piano very decently to people who want to play the piano a bit. She earns her living, she does what she does quite properly. She has a place in her society. Why should I say to her: 'You must be a Rostropovich or a Richter?' I don't see why you must be Richter to teach in a little town. He wouldn't know what on earth to do there.

So you mustn't construct universal classifications. Each individual poses a particular problem. You must dare to choose, but on what basis? Talent is not necessarily linked to the quality of a man; you can be a great musician and at the same time a dreadful, vice-ridden person — vices pay for human weaknesses — what is unacceptable is mediocrity.

When a child or even an adult comes to consult you, what happens?

I make him work at solfeggio with Mademoiselle Dieudonné, and I teach him harmony and counterpoint.

That is, you teach technique?

A 'draconian' technique!

Can you give him both technique and élan?

Ah now, *he* has to have the *élan!*

I've never taught many children, there has been little occasion and then such talented cases that they prove nothing. But one day, a child — Jean Françaix — was to come for his first harmony lesson and I said to myself, 'How am I going to conduct this?' It kept me awake, I fretted all night. When he arrived, I said,

'You know, Jean, today we are going to work on chords . . .'.

'Ah yes, like this . . .', and he played me a chord, with his childlike air, because he was really just a child. At the end of two months I said to his mother, 'Madame, I don't know why we are wasting our time making him work on harmony, he knows harmony. I don't know how, but he knows it, he was born knowing it. Let's do counterpoint.'

And the same thing happened again?

No, he had to work at it, because counterpoint is always an immense intellectual struggle. The same thing happened with a Roumanian student, a great pianist, who had assimilated the treatise on harmony in a flash. With the piano, you must make efforts before mastering a technique. But in harmony she divined everything. She became a great pianist and never developed into a composer. Which was just as well, because she wasn't made for that.

Are you sure that what you teach is of direct use to each student who comes to you?

Of course not. Recently someone asked me to provide a list of my American pupils. I said it would be impossible. The poor people here who investigated the matter came up with an impressive number. Just since 1934, I believe, six hundred American students. Among those there are some I can barely recall. Others shine out in all they have done; in their characters, in their lives, in themselves, as marvellous people. Others fall between.

Should I have discouraged those who were not first-class? I don't think so. I believe it's necessary to fulfil certain essential conditions, and afterwards each has a place for a specific function. You must take your actions to the limit of your aspirations.

I had a dear old woman from the country who used to polish the furniture and do the washing. She would come to the sitting-room and knock very timidly: 'I know Mademoiselle doesn't like to be disturbed, but it shines so brightly that Mademoiselle should see it.' And I would go and admire the piece that shone. And then one day she said to me,

'You know, Mademoiselle, I don't want to do the washing any more.'

'Look here, you're old, you should rest now. You have worked hard enough all your life.'

'It's not that, it's because of Mademoiselle's students.'

'Was someone not polite to you?'

'Oh! They're all very nice, these young ladies, but you know, in the days when I used to wash Mademoiselle's blouse, or Madame Lamy's, or Madame Duval's, I knew who they belonged to and I would think of Madame Duval, Madame Lamy or Mademoiselle. Now they're all the same kind of blouse. You wash one, then the next, and you think you haven't washed the first because it's just the same. Well, that's boring now!'

'You don't know what a great lesson you have taught us about art.'

If everyone wrote the same type of fugue with the same number of beats, with the same counterpoint, it would be deadly! Each gifted person's fugue is unpredictable. It might be a failure, but it will be inventive. Sometimes I'm tired, but when talented people arrive, I can stay up till midnight. My weariness vanishes! On the other hand, if there's a pupil who hasn't done enough work, I say: 'I am not here to make you work. If you don't want to work, don't work, I don't care. I'm only interested in you at the moment when you come alive. At that moment, I try to live with you and to help you live.'

The marvellous thing is to admit and welcome children or adolescents like my little chap Emile Naoumoff, who is fourteen. At Wednesday's class, I constantly have to say to him 'No, not you . . .'. I ask a question: 'No, not you.' Because he knows, he has the answer straight away, before anyone else. So nobody speaks up. I spend my time saying 'Not you . . .'.

He was like that when he arrived. He's an exceptional person; he played in October with the Berlin orchestra; eight days later he came first in calculus at school. He was as happy to have come first in calculus as to have played his concerto in Berlin. Playing gave him pleasure, but I think coming first gave him still more pleasure because it surprised him, whereas playing the concerto seemed natural.

In England, at the Yehudi Menuhin School

The essential thing with gifted children is to induce them to be themselves, to give them a vocabulary and not to stand in their way. That is my great struggle and my great hope. But adults are often quite awkward. When I left the Conservatoire in 1904, people made a fuss of me and pointed me out; 'It's the little Boulanger who won three first prizes in the same week!' I was very timid then — I don't show it anymore but I still am — and I was in despair. I didn't know what to say.

Similarly, when very young, Idil Biret played in a recital for two pianos with Wilhelm Kempff. A triumph! The next morning I said to her, 'You played so well, I should like to do something for you. What would you like?' She was eleven and a half or twelve.

'I would love to go and hear Edwin Fischer.'

'Very well; I happen to have a box.'

At the concert, Idil and I were in the box. The first lady arrives: 'Ah, it's the little girl . . . this genius . . . this . . . !'

At first Idil smiled but little by little she retreated to the back of the box, and when the tenth person came up saying 'Ah, the genius, what a marvel!' she shut up completely. And when the people had left, she said to me, 'It's funny, these grown-ups say exactly what shouldn't be said.' She was right.

One day we went to dine with a friend of my parents. I must have been four years old. We were in Viroflay and there were apricots on the table. I adored apricots. My parents left me quite free in such matters. I took an apricot and my parents' friend said: 'A well brought-up little girl doesn't serve herself before she has been served.' I said to myself, 'You are nasty,' and I really thought she was horrid. Instead of giving me good advice, she made me feel guilty. I was so happy at home it had no effect, I found her horrid and that was that.

I knew someone whose son spoke a rough kind of Russian. A Russian lady came to see his mother once, and when the little boy began to jabber away, the lady exclaimed, 'Oh what a funny accent he has!' He didn't speak another word of Russian for twenty years.

You can squash people. One remark made in a certain way, on the other hand, can encourage and give confidence. One must tell the truth, but with a view to inspiring confidence and liberating the inner self; it is very difficult, and collective education doesn't allow for it. If I only dealt with groups of students, I would be obliged to submit them to a discipline which would be blind to individuals. Thus it's always necessary to have one-to-one contact, because no one is like anyone else. He is himself.

There is a limit to the truth you can tell; but you can, if you are convinced that there is perceptible progress, instil confidence. Some years ago a lady came to see me: 'Mademoiselle, our daughter, who is retarded, has a mad dream. She wants to have lessons with you. We know she can't make any progress, it won't do her any good, but she already has such an unhappy life! Would you give her some lessons?'

I replied, 'Madame, I'm afraid it would require a measure of patience that I'm not sure I possess.'

'Mademoiselle, do try, for pity's sake.'

Fortunately her father was transferred, they left after a few months. I held out. But I said to myself, 'I cannot permit myself a moment of impatience because she can do nothing.'

I used to give her lessons as I would send a packet of sweets to a sick child; if I hadn't done it that way, I wouldn't have been able to provide her with even the illusion of joy. But that had nothing to do with teaching.

A Mentor

Do you know that text of Valéry's: 'In the past, one imitated mastery, today one searches for singularity.'

It is cruel, for one is singular because one cannot be like everyone else. One isn't singular by choice.

I desperately try to make a pupil understand that he must express what he wants; I don't mind whether he agrees with me or not, so long as he can tell me: 'This is what I want to say, this is what I love, this is what I'm looking for.' Today, we are at a fascinating point because everything is in question. Those who provide an answer are those who find a new language which isn't to be discussed, or approved, or rejected: it simply exists. We know already that there are some who make themselves understand and others who seek to do so, and others who haven't much to say and are looking for something to say. But that has been the case in the past, too. The difference is that previously there was such an established style that if the music was trivial, it was nevertheless intelligible; whereas in a time of experiment, when language is handled by people who don't know what they're doing, it makes for the vague in the vague, the uncertain in the uncertain.

When my students compose, I prefer them to be mistaken if they must make mistakes, but to remain natural and free rather than wishing to appear other than what they are. I remember a day when Stravinsky was dining here. He took his neighbour at the table by the lapels, violently! His neighbour, crushed, said to him; 'But Monsieur Stravinsky, I don't know why we're talking like this, I agree with you.' And Stravinsky exclaimed furiously, 'Yes, but not for the right reasons, so you are wrong.'

You can have good or bad reasons for searching. If you search in order to hide your inadequacy, you're wrong. If you are looking in order to say what you really want to say, you're right. And so it's very important for a teacher first of all to let his pupil play as he wishes, write as he wishes; and then to be ruthless on questions of discipline.

The student who has completely assimilated Hindemith's book, *Elementary Training for Musicians* — a pedagogical masterpiece — cannot be stumped by any question of rhythm, harmony or counterpoint. It is a book of pure theory, indispensable to all musicians and containing remarkable exercises. Hindemith knew about music in such an amazing way that sometimes it is difficult to distinguish the composer from the teacher. The whole of his work is made up of very beautiful writing and the most exquisite combinations. But despite his very curious and analytic mind, I wonder whether his teaching hasn't influenced his work as a composer. Certainly there is a difference between the Hindemith of *Mathis der Maler* and that of *Marienleben*, but the development isn't very marked. The second version of *Marienleben* seems to me, in some of the pieces that I love deeply, a betrayal of his original thought. I say this in all humility.

He himself said of his educational books that they had led to bad Hindemith being written by many young composers, and sometimes by himself. On the necessity and danger of convention: without conventions, you don't have a framework, and without a framework you're lost, you lose your balance. But you fall over too if you abandon yourself to convention or to fashion.

A great work, I believe, is made out of a combination of obedience and liberty. Such a work satisfies the mind, together with that curious thing which is artistic emotion. Stravinsky said, 'If I were permitted everything, I would be lost in the abyss of liberty.' On the one hand he knew the limits, on the other he ceaselessly extended them.

If we look at the history of human production we note that there is a kind of tacit and profound accord between what has been achieved and what has been transcended. Take a work of the importance of Bach's *Well-Tempered Clavier;* the obedience is such that when Bach makes a decision, it always corresponds to a rule, to a convention that can be explained in clear terms. Thus he begins by obeying. But within that obedience, he is absolutely free. He doesn't submit to obedience, he chooses it.

Have you ever been shocked by a pupil, or by a work fundamentally new in relation to what you appreciate in the works you know?

I don't know what you mean by the word 'shocked'. You might use the word 'struck', but the word 'shocked' implies refusal, rejection; 'struck' means expectation. And it is very different to confront a work you don't know yet, or a work in which you have to recognize some worth, while secretly saying to yourself, 'That's a trend which I would never follow.' That's a matter of personal taste.

Can't culture allow us to pass beyond personal taste to see that an object is beautiful? Do I have to buy it or to own it? No, but I am able to see that it is beautiful.

Perhaps there are some theories of musical technique that correspond more to your own taste than others?

If it were a matter of my own principles, that would be important because of the work I could do. But I am incapable of writing anything valuable. I realized at twenty that I wasn't a composer. Thus my preferences are of no account. I trust that a certain approach to grammar and to the form of language goes beyond personal taste. To what extent are you not influenced? I'm not entirely certain on this score. I've never said to a pupil: 'You are mistaken because I am right,' rather, 'I think that you are mistaken, but not necessarily because I am right.'

One of my pupils — I believe he's a born composer — lately brought me a piece I find very complex, not at all to my taste but extremely interesting. I conveyed my approval to him, and my hope that he would take that direction. The same boy, several days afterwards, returned with a piece I found horrible, and I said to him: 'Listen, my dear, I am not sure that I was right when I liked your piece the other day and I'm not sure that I'm right to detest this one, but I am sure that I would never play this one again, except to test my judgement and try to know it better in order to overcome my dislike.'

I hope my influence works in favour of the need for rigour and order. But in the area of style, if I exercise an influence it is despite myself and against my will. If I am faced with a foreigner and I try to make him French, I think that I'm bound to fail. I say to my Japanese pupils, 'I beg you to remain Japanese and become universal in other respects.' I endeavour to make them recognize their origins and avoid making them — under the pretext of their coming to work in Paris — imitation Parisians. Universality isn't rootlessness, and you do feel that Brahms isn't Neapolitan, nor Monteverdi Swedish.

Similarly, if you take a work like the *Musical Offering*, you wouldn't dream of dancing to it, at least not yet. Perhaps they'll dance to it one day, but the work doesn't carry in itself the idea of dancing, whereas you cannot hear the least page of Manuel de Falla without feeling the dance, without sensing Spain.

What is the exact function of your analysis course?

To make people listen. To make them hear music no longer as a vertical phenomenon, but as a horizontal one. The rest eludes analysis.

Why do you take as your object of analysis the fugues of Bach, rather than the scholastic fugues of a local Academician?

The latter seem to me empty, a form with nothing but the appearance of form, the former full of inexhaustible treasures. I think it's essential to distinguish the area you can analyse — that is the craft — from what escapes our speculation and makes the saints, the heroes, the geniuses. They are another race.

It is very paradoxical: your profession, your principal occupation, is to analyse. Then why this avoidance of analysis at the same time?

All that is beyond my mind, my reach, because it requires verbal ingenuity and knowledge that I don't have. But I'm intuitive. I thank God when I think that these values are mysteriously intelligible to me. And I'd go further: I don't like people to try to make things too clear to me. If I like someone, I don't want to examine how many bacteria, drugs, vitamins he might have, invisible to me. I sense certain things. If I had both intuition and reason, that would be superb; but I don't feel that remarkable. I am someone who knows her profession, who has given advice that has allowed people to acquire basic techniques, to listen well, to understand properly, to transcribe, rehearse, remember. The role of teacher seems to me a modest one. To someone who wants to work, I put the question: 'Are you able to see, are you able to listen, are you able to remember?' If I have helped to make that possible, I have given what is at my disposal. But to provide a great philosophy, that I cannot claim to do.

A Lecture Course

Each year you choose a list of works to be analysed in your Wednesday course. I have in front of me this year's list, which seems very intriguing. There are some surprising combinations, and I must admit I find it difficult to grasp the dominant theme.

Naturally you divide the year into three terms, however there's an element common to all three, Bach's Well-Tempered Clavier. *Yet the first term begins with an anonymous 'Tantum Ergo'.*

In an age characterized by accretion, I have tried to show what the peace of Gregorian melody was, that pure line which cannot even bear accompaniment. When I think of the idea of plain-chant current when I was a child, and how it was harmonized — a mad notion but it was done — I can hardly believe it! Music founded on Gregorian chant very soon gave way to combinations of two voices, then several voices, right up to Tallis's motets for forty voices.

Clearly someone writing for one voice, and someone writing for two, eighteen or forty voices, has different aims: can the one writing a motet for forty voices follow all forty throughout the piece? I rather doubt it . . . Nobody so far has been able to hear them all, therefore I'm still waiting to see. Someone had better hurry up and tell me because I mightn't be able to wait much longer. In any case, I have strong doubts.

When was Tallis writing?

At the same time as those marvellous composers Byrd, Dowland, Morley, the 'Tudor Musicians'. Fortunately one mad day I was able to buy the ten volumes of *Tudor Church Music.* I owe them some marvellous hours. Then you come to the great period of Paiestrina, Orlando di Lasso, finally the great Victoria in Spain and Cabezón for the organ. Time goes by and I've had much joy in the company of the English.

must be reintroduced into the creation itself: it is the technique which ensures that a good weaver never produces bad cloth. Talent without genius is nothing much, but genius without talent is nothing at all.

Do you remember what Cocteau said: 'True tears are not drawn from our eyes by a sad page, but by the miracle of a word in its proper place.' The chosen word which no other word can replace.

You could ask: is it possible to free ourselves of certain structures; could we build a language outside everything we call logic? I own that I'm so preoccupied with music, I leave men who deal with words to discuss and decide on that.

André Malraux didn't have the technique of a specialist in the arts that interested him. But what an admirable technique with words! On the other hand, Malraux's language annoys many artists, since he transposes into a very general area of expression what was, at the outset, the domain of a technical idiom.

Valéry often said to me, 'You are lucky; for you, putting a note on a line or between the lines changes everything; we have nothing so precise.'

It is disturbing how everyone can do the same thing, and nothing comes from 999 out of 1000; but one of them will say something unforgettable.

That one in a thousand both invents and knows the properties of language, a knowledge which leaves the way free for the expression of the involuntary and unconscious in creation. No one would pretend that Bach's 220 cantatas are all masterpieces of the same order; but they are more of the order of masterpieces than of mediocrity! Such is their level of technique. But I think a masterpiece is unconscious; I don't at all believe that Bach began his *St Matthew Passion* by saying to himself 'Now I am going to write a masterpiece.' He tried to complete it by the set deadline, to conform to the conditions of performance, the number of musicians, the time available — in other words, the practical factors, the pair of appropriate shoes, which don't squeak or slip. If these shoes are exceptional, it seems to me he doesn't know it himself. For someone who can rely on technique, it is the commission and the circumstances that shape the work. Obviously if I write a waltz, it won't do as a requiem. Still, it could be that I was burying some quite genial fellow who had said (this happened to one of my students, that's why I mention it), 'I have had a delightful life and I want for my funeral music that has given me pleasure.'

And so my student, a very well-educated and serious Protestant, was obliged to play just after the religious ceremony half-an-hour's racket that the deceased had enjoyed and which, when he came to bid his friends farewell for the last time, he had wanted them to hear. After all, it wasn't harming anyone. It was rather surprising, all the same!

What is true in a work of art, a man or a landscape? How do we know we're perceiving it? In certain people there's an insatiable hunger to discover it. One day Herr Johann Sebastian Bach presented himself to play at the court of Frederick the Great, who provided him with a theme on which to improvise. Going home, probably not entirely satisfied with his improvisation, anxious better to understand how to manage the means he used or which in certain cases he forged himself, he wrote on the same theme the 'Ricercare' in six parts and the canons of the *Musical Offering*. These canons are a freak of intellectual interest and pose insoluble problems. He found a solution, but today, at this end of the twentieth century, certain canons of the *Musical Offering* can still be read in two different ways: we can't be sure. The same thing happens in the *Art of Fugue* with the fugue that can be entirely reversed. It is intellectually monstrous. You can play it backwards and upside down and everything continues to work. Do you realize what that represents in self-control, in unlimited technique! However, the interest of these works isn't purely intellectual, because their author is an immense musician, a man who — fragile as he was, miserable as he was — had prescience, a notion of the mysteries surrounding him, and opened them to us and made us feel them.

I haven't studied mathematics, but I should say that in maths there comes a stage when you can no longer calculate, where you enter into infinity. I believe that in the same way a masterpiece fulfills a set of conditions which we cannot measure, which escapes us, which is beyond ourselves, which ensures a balance between the means and what emerges; although the creator may not be aware of it.

One day I was talking to Stravinsky. He was explaining that he ordered shirts from Lanvin with such and such collars and sleeves. I was suddenly struck by the banality of the topic, despite the personality that introduced it. I said, 'When I think that you have exercised influence all over the world and here we are talking about your shirts. It's rather odd, to say the least.' He replied, 'I don't consider it odd at all.' Then, in the conditional and very slowly — when he spoke seriously, he spoke slowly — 'I only know how difficult it is to try to do what I should like to do.'

In every work of an artist worthy of the name, there is technique, and then something extra, not learnt.

An academic work may be perfectly accomplished; you know it, you admire it, but you cannot love it because it doesn't contain that element I can't define; what marks the difference between well-made music and a simple melody by Schubert, so simple that there's nothing to it, just innocence and an irresistibly spontaneous movement that makes it a masterpiece. Recently someone read me a letter from a friend of Schubert who wrote: 'We liked him a great deal, we found him very good company, but we had no idea, we didn't realize what a genius he was.' That is so disturbing. Faced with genius and a masterpiece, I confess to you that I'm embarrassed. In fact I don't know. I know and I don't know, because my certainty doesn't rest on the certainty of reason. It is reasonable in so far as I note that the music is well written, well orchestrated, well constructed. But the moment it passes into something else, it becomes mysterious. Since I am a believer, everything seems mysterious to me. It seems mysterious to be born; how am I going to greet death? Tranquilly, not tranquilly, with fear, without fear? I've no idea, I've never yet been in danger of it. I accept this curious mystery: I am. They also exist, but in their own prodigious measure, those men who, whatever motivates them, whatever their means, manage to convince us through their work down the centuries.

There is, alas, some music I don't like, though I recognize it is brilliant of its kind. It may be entirely successful, deserving respect, yet not correspond to what I'm able to feel. That doesn't prevent me from knowing the score perhaps better than a score I really like. I don't care for Alban Berg's *Lulu*; I'm probably wrong, but I don't like *Lulu*. And yet whenever *Lulu* is played on the radio I listen to it. The dreadful thing last time wasn't that I disliked it, but that it bored me. I said to myself, 'What a comedown!' Because not to love is still an image of loving, but indifference, boredom! If I'm bored, it is because I'm bored with myself. I thereby condemn myself.

Presences

Pupils from the New World

You have moulded American musicians by the hundred, there can't be a town in the North American continent without one of your pupils at least among its inhabitants.

I have had a lot of American pupils, that's true. It's easy to forget that fifty years ago, no one knew of American music, it wasn't an expression you used. There's been an enormous change since then, and today Mr Copland comes to conduct in London, in Rome, in Paris; Mr Bernstein conducts, and his works are played all over the world.

The term 'American musician' is no longer unusual. It was unknown before for specific reasons: a number of foreign musicians had settled in America, but no musicians had been trained entirely there. This situation was linked to political, religious and racial questions; the artistic culture of America developed relatively late. The amalgam of these elements seems to have been achieved first in America through popular music, supplied by black men who had a particular talent for music but were hardly American in origin.

Of course, very few of us are pure French for generations back without any dilution; most of us are descended from parents of diverse origins, there's a mixture. But this mixing has gone on for such a long time that, as a wine that's quite old is more itself, more recognizable than an absolutely new wine, we can easily assert our identity. A tree has roots that establish themselves deep in the earth and the process requires time. The musical heritage of black Americans still constitutes an essential compost. Beginning from that, and little by little, American musicians have created an entirely new concept by using old methods. America has managed to generate a very advanced civilization without roots; it had to create simultaneously the fruit and the root; it has, I believe, succeeded to a very great extent.

Many of the great names of American music came to work with you.

At about the same period I became acquainted with Aaron Copland, Walter Piston, Roger Sessions and Virgil Thomson. Elliott Carter didn't come until later.

America was unloaded on you in the 1920s!

Yes, in a sense. One of them, Walter Piston, has just died. He was gifted with an extraordinary delicacy, over and above his talent. One day I received a letter from him: 'As you perhaps realize, I left Paris owing you a hundred dollars' — I had no idea he owed me anything whatsoever. 'I am sending them to you with my apologies for being so slow. I know that I cannot offer you the interest, you would not accept it, but I am enclosing an additional sum which you can give to a pupil who needs it.' That was marvellous. Others never even think of bringing you a violet; not that they aren't nice, it just doesn't occur to them.

His vocation was to teach, and he thought that in order to build on a solid basis he should go over everything, harmony, counterpoint, everything. At the beginning he didn't want to come to see me, because he didn't want to work with a woman; when he finally arrived, I said to him, 'I quite understand, I would have been as anxious as you, I would have gone to see a man at the outset, but here you are. So much the better.' And we became great friends.

He became a very important composer and was professor at Harvard for years, as Leonard Bernstein was subsequently. I didn't know Leonard Bernstein until he'd finished his studies at Harvard, but he was one of those pupils you teach little because they intuit everything: a prodigious gift, a many-sided personality, assimilating all the methods, with an incomparable freshness and the ability to adapt gracefully. I am particularly fond of him, he is so warm and sensitive. He still gives me the pleasure of his visits when he passes through Paris, and sometimes plays me his latest compositions. But I've never presumed to claim him as one of my pupils.

Nearly half a century ago another great American conductor, Walter Damrosch, invited me to come and play the organ in New York; I was then also invited by Koussevitsky in Boston. Aaron Copland was my pupil at the time and then totally unknown. I thought it would be an opportunity for such a young man to make himself heard. After Damrosch and Koussevitsky had agreed, I said to Copland: 'If you could be ready by the first of September, and you are interested in writing a piece for organ and orchestra, I could assure you it would be performed in New York and Boston. Only if you are ready by the first of September, though, not the second!'

On the first of September I had the score, finished, copied, all in order.

We arrived in New York. At the end of the concert — I like it immensely, this little symphony for organ and orchestra — I never discovered Damrosch's motive, probably he'd been scared by the modernism of the work — anyway, he turned to the audience and said, 'Ladies and Gentlemen, if a man of twenty-three can write a work like this, he might, before he's thirty, kill his parents!' In jest! half in jest, half in earnest! The audience of course reacted, there was a great stir . . . Copland's reputation was made.

Pupils from the Old World

Aside from the Americans, I'm hard put to tell you if the largest group of those who worked with me here came from England — composers of very great talent like Lennox Berkeley, or more recently Edwin Roxburgh and Malcolm Singer — or from Poland. Among my Polish pupils I've kept many marvellous friends, people who were very promising and who've fulfilled their promise: Mycielski, and Rudzinsky, who still seems a child to me because he was born in 1935. In any case he's a very active, very valuable composer.

Those names are relatively unknown here. Lutoslawski or Penderecki is far better known.

To think that a certain generation already finds Penderecki old-fashioned! Some consider that he repeats himself, which can happen when someone has real personality: his music is recognizable, and he's reproached for it. Penderecki has his system, but he is a great musician.

Did he work with you?

No, not at all. I can't call him my pupil. No advertisement there for the rue Ballu!

Actually when I say he didn't work with me at all, that's not quite true. During his stay in Paris, he came here sometimes. I know that I immediately registered him as someone very gifted, a real creative force.

The stream of students from eastern Europe doesn't cease. Even today, you accept new ones.

One day a lady arrived with a charming little boy, really little, he wasn't nine; his outfit, his little tie, everything perfectly in order.

He sat down at the piano, played a piece of Bach very nicely and then stopped: 'I would also like you to hear one of my compositions,' he said to me. A composition that wasn't at all freakish, put together very inventively, unbelievably energetic and authoritative!

Thus we began, and little Emile Naoumoff, who is Bulgarian, is one of the gifts of my old age. He's now been with me five years and his personality as a composer is developing naturally, without his being tied to any school.

From the beginning, I said to him: 'Never do what I might say to you in a weak moment if it seems to you I'm mistaken.' A few of his works could be the object of some formal criticism. I am determined not to do that, in order to let him develop. Sometimes I ask myself, 'Let's see, is the music he's writing influenced by Stravinsky? No. By Bartok? No. By Shostakovich? Perhaps a bit, but not entirely.' I let him speak his own language. He does what he wants. When he does a harmony exercise, I make him go over a correction six times, until it is perfect from the academic point of view; but when he composes, I want him to be absolutely free.

At thirteen, already an old pupil of the house, confiding a great secret, he told me, 'I've composed an *opéra-bouffe.*'

'With whose libretto?'

'Mine; I'm working on the orchestration and I'll show it to you when it's finished.'

His opera was a vigorous composition, precise and very natural. He recently gave a performance of it. He took rehearsals kindly, patiently and firmly, with the astonishing authority of an old hand, giving himself over to it entirely.

In fact, the case of little Naoumoff is fairly astonishing. I knew a similar case with Idel Biret who arrived in Paris at the age of seven and a half, unable to read music but playing Mozart's Concerto in C major as though she would never play it better. It was played by a great artist who happened to be a little girl of seven and a half, unable to read music. You played her a piece once or twice and she know it thoroughly. She couldn't make a mistake in harmony; she understood everything. Naoumoff understands everything too.

It seems to me very hard to predict a pianist's future, given that musical life, musical activity, the consumption of music in the years to come will take forms we don't know. For a composer, isn't it even more complex? Aren't you concerned for a young composer of thirteen or fourteen?

He was born a musician, he writes music, he cannot not write it. If I'm concerned, that won't affect anything that's inevitable.

Lipatti

Lipatti was an angel on earth. You cannot imagine what he was: noble, profound, gay, right up to his death; he knew very well that there was a time-limit, a limit without remission.

It was very hard for him to go, and yet he was ready. I don't need to tell you that he was one of the greatest pianists ever, the very image of a complete musician. But the man! Once I arrived in Geneva to see him since I knew that time was limited. Already he didn't go out any more. He said to me:

'We're going to the doctor.'

'Why?'

'Because you're run down. I've made an appointment for you.'

He'd set up the whole thing with the doctor, he'd reserved a room with a balcony in a rest-home. Everything was organized. It's true I was very tired, and he attached importance to those days of rest for me although he himself was dying. There was something so moving in this person who loved life, who gave his wonderful concerts, who made incomparably beautiful recordings, at a time when he was having to undergo blood transfusions.

Around the same time, Ansermet had conducted the Schu-

With Dinu Lipatti

mann Concerto for him. He told me afterwards that he wept throughout the concert, seeing before him someone obviously dying, who played sublimely.

Well, let's forget all sorts of illness to remember the incomparable radiance he emanated from the piano, over his audience, over himself. I think the bit of extra emotion that comes from the fact of his illness should be forgotten, and we should think of Lipatti living, of the great artist. There was never any ill-feeling round Lipatti. He was disarming in his frailty.

You made recordings with him?

Yes, we played a great deal together. I succeeded Paul Dukas in the composition class at the Ecole Normale, and this is where I came across Lipatti. As soon as I saw this gift, this thrilling and intelligent musicality in control of itself, I was overcome, quite overwhelmed. Equally by his generous, serious nature. A great person. He was a godson of Enesco, with whom I'd been a student at the Conservatoire. Their spiritual relationship was profound. I think I remember, though I can't be absolutely sure, that Enesco wrote to me about him, but it was Alfred Cortot who sent him to me, as it was Alfred Cortot who sent me Igor Markevitch.

Markevitch

I remember the first day Markevitch came into my class; he must have been nearly fifteen. I had asked my counterpoint pupils to listen to a four-part counterpoint and I had asked whether anyone could play it back to me. The usual response to this kind of question was dead silence. But little Markevitch got up, and with extreme politeness said:

'If you would allow me, Mademoiselle, I should like to try.'

'It's impossible, you haven't done counterpoint.'

To everyone's astonishment, perhaps even to his own, he played back the entire counterpoint from memory. By the end of the class, half the students were at his feet, and the others would never forgive him. Too superior, too refined, too cultivated.

Still almost a child, Markevitch was very assured: you asked a question, he knew the answer and gave it. The others were sometimes a bit annoyed at him.

Igor Markevitch was known first as a composer?

Yes. Why he stopped composing, or showing his compositions, I don't know. I'm not keeping a secret, I am faced with one, which I can't begin to fathom.

It seems to me that your decision to give up composing is just as baffling.

That concerns nobody.

Markevitch's decision of the same order.

The same order as what?

As your own decision.

Oh not at all; in my case I realized that my music was useless. Markevitch could please himself or not, but whatever his motivation, he couldn't believe that his music was insignificant. The *Psalm* and *Icarus* are major scores. They have such strength and originality.

I honestly don't know what happened. As far as I'm concerned, it was a great tragedy. He wrote music with such a personal stamp, music which no one can make use of.

He is one of those people who is surrounded by ignorance in those around him, though they have everything to gain and profit from his presence. You had everything to gain from knowing Markevitch better. He's known and acclaimed as a magnificent conductor; but people are ignorant and totally fail to understand other aspects of his personality. That doesn't really matter, he is Markevitch.

Igor Markevitch, Nadia Boulanger, Dinu Lipatti

Lili

She was born in Paris on 21 August 1893. From her earliest years until she was sixteen, she roamed about the world of music, singing, working at various instruments, but not deciding on anything. What inner world did she build, this curious little girl with a character so precociously defined? At sixteen, she committed herself to the course she would never abandon. Her mind was made up, she would be a composer, and she began the necessary technical studies, crowned by a Premier Grand Prix de Rome, the first awarded to a woman. She was then nineteen and working non-stop at her *oeuvre*. She had already encountered death, at the age of six when our father died. Marked — illuminated — by sadness, she devoted herself to exceedingly grave concerns — too grave for such a delicate, fragile girl. She was aware that her life would be brief, her time measured. Much calmer than we are today, talking about it, she looked ahead to her own death. She still had everything to say, but she had to abandon the projects that were her very life, leave what she loved. On 15 March 1918 her suffering came to an end. She had never shown the slightest tendency to rebel, only the overwhelming need to say what she had to say. She took care of herself, not in order to live longer, but in the hope of saying what remained for her to say. This wasn't arrogance, simply the expression of the music that welled up in her more compellingly than any outside pressures. She wrote because she had something to say, and she had to say it in an inaccessible language, the language of art.

The artist creates an object which is independent of its creator and of those who contemplate it. The object in itself becomes important. We experience this with all works that command our attention: it is the work that dominates. We say Leonardo, but we see the paintings. We say Michelangelo, we see the sculptures, but in an impersonal way because it's the work that counts. Still, it takes time to forget Lili Boulanger's very sad fate, to turn our attention exclusively to her work. She has sealed her work in silence. She did not want to lay bare her thoughts because only the music counted. That said, I wonder why there is a certain reluctance to acknowledge her place in musical history. Perhaps it's because she was on the fringes of what was happening at the time she was writing. And further there was no Cocteau to launch her, as he did Radiguet. But she is the first important woman composer in history. Her principal works show a sureness

Lili and Nadia Boulanger

of touch, a sureness of form, which are really little short of miraculous since they were composed when she was at an age when it is easy to proceed by trial and error. You have the impression that there is no trial and error and that straightaway she achieves a certain sublimity of form, through what she seeks and the way in which she realizes it. Nothing that was not noble thrived in the presence of Lili Boulanger. I don't mean to suggest that people are insensitive to this, but they are not used to taking her life so seriously. Thanks to Igor Markevitch, Yehudi Menuhin, Clifford Curzon, Eric Tappy and Jean Françaix — thanks also to some anonymous, devoted American and English friends — some of her compositions can still be heard. Have I failed her in not doing more myself?

The day my father announced, 'You have a little sister', I went to stand in front of the cradle where this little sister was. I was six, and I felt I had been entrusted with her protection. Very soon it was I who was protected, because she was stronger, had more energy, a greater faith, in a different measure from mine.

I have scruples that I haven't overcome about the publication of certain of her letters. There was not the shadow of a secret in my sister's life, but I feel that if I published her correspondence, she'd say to me, 'What! I wrote them to you and you are showing them to all the world!' Perhaps I'm wrong, but I'm in an awkward position. She represents the best, the most intimate, the most profound elements in my life. Only silence seems to suit these feelings.

Stravinsky

I had included Stravinsky's *Introitus* for men's voices in a concert programme, and I wanted it to be played twice.

To space out these two performances, I had asked Pierre Fresnay to come and read some bits of Valéry's 'Cimetière Marin'. The text fitted in marvellously. It was very impressive. It had always seemed to me that secret correspondences existed between the composer and the writer, though they were such different men.

We often had little dinner parties at which Valéry and

Stravinsky were both present. Only one subject provoked silence on one side and outbursts on the other: the subject of religion. Stravinsky was fanatically religious, while Valéry never spoke about religion. Stravinsky was steeped in ideas of sin, of God, Valéry was silent, he would resume conversation later. But he never asked, 'How can you possibly believe all that?' He felt that he was confronted by something true, authentic. And the authentic inspired his respect.

Valéry lived five minutes away from us at Gargenville. Sometimes I used to meet him on the path; he would stop. While he spoke, he described circles with his cane. And as he approached the essence of his subject, its inner truth, the circle would tighten. He only retained and confided the essentials.

Nor was Stravinsky a man to confide something easily, and whether in his letters — almost always very short — or in conversation, his confidences were given in very few words.

I know no man more loyal to his deepest feelings, more loyal to his faith. Pope John XXIII said to me several times how much he had been struck by Stravinsky's humility. He had known him since hearing the work Stravinsky had come to conduct in San Marco; the future John XXIII was then Patriarch of Venice.

Some years later, the Pope invited him — to his great astonishment ('He knows perfectly well that I'm not Catholic!') — to conduct his own Mass in the Sistine Chapel, and I received a cable from Stravinsky: 'Going to be ennobled by the Holy Father. Imagine my pride.' At that time Stravinsky wasn't Doctor *honoris causa* anywhere. He had no title, except perhaps for a kind of law diploma dating from his twenties. He had always refused everything. But he considered that the greatest honour of his life.

I knew his charming old mother well. She was a little surprised at having a son so different from herself. To see Stravinsky with his mother was one of the most touching things imaginable: first, the heels together with that characteristic noise, pac! and they clicked. And if she didn't ask him to sit down, he remained standing. He was fifty years old, he was the glory of the whole world. But he remained standing in front of his mother, as his sons did before him. It was a Russian tradition and the tradition of their family.

A few years before his death, he went back to Russia for several concerts. On his way he came through Paris and said to me: 'My mind tells me that I must go, but I'm frightened.' He had left Russia half a century before and feared re-establishing contact after so many years, finding all he'd passionately loved unrecognizable. If I were lucky enough to be a writer, I would write a book — which will never appear — on tenderness in the works of Stravinsky.

Just think of 'Eglogue II' in the *Duo Concertant*, of the 'Dithyrambe,' that inexplicably beautiful masterpiece: a few measures, a line, and you attain the sublime. With Paul Makanovitzky, I've experimented several times playing the beginning of Bach's Sonata in E for violin and clavier and following it immediately with 'Dithyrambe'. They link up in such a marvellous way that time is obliterated. That restores memory in the present, the present to memory and to the past. Consider too the joyous outpouring of the 'Gigue', in which you perceive so deeply an old, intimate relationship with the Russian soul.

*But isn't it necessary, particularly in Stravinsky's case, to distance the music from its composer? Isn't it Stravinsky who says that music expresses nothing?**

He protected himself. Above all he needed protection and shunned familiarity. His strength was so great that it naturally isolated him. Not wishing anyone to pry into his private life, he'd say, 'There are no feelings' and leave you standing outside. One can close a door for two reasons: because you need a degree of isolation, but also to avoid a breath of air.

When I'm listening to Bach, I don't say to myself: 'He had two wives and twenty-one children.' If I listen to *The Rite of Spring*, I

---

* 'The phenomenon of music is given to us with the sole purpose of establishing an order in things, including and particularly, the co-ordination between *man* and *time*. To be put into practice, its indispensable and single requirement is construction. Once the construction is completed, this order has been attained, and there is nothing more to be said. It would be futile to look for, or to expect, anything else from it. It is precisely this construction, this achieved order, which produces in us a unique emotion, which has nothing in common with our ordinary sensations and our responses to the impressions of daily life. One could not better define the sensation music produces than by saying that it is identical with that evoked by contemplation of the interplay of architectural forms. Goethe thoroughly understood that when he called architecture 'petrified music'. I consider my music, in its essence, incapable of expressing a feeling, an attitude, a psychological state, a natural phenomenon, or whatever. Expression has never been the immanent property of music. If, as is nearly always the case, music seems to express something, it is only an illusion and not reality. It is simply an additional element that by inveterate, tacit convention, we have seized on and imposed as a rule, a protocol. And which, through habit or unconsciously, we have come to confuse with its essence.' — Igor Stravinsky, *Chronicle of my Life* (ch. IV).

don't reflect, 'To think that I know him, that I like him very much, that he is such a personality, that I know all his family, all the people around him!' Perhaps afterwards, but not during the work; when I listen, I'm not thinking of Catherine nor of Theodore nor even of Igor himself.

There is something that I could never have done, though we were deeply attached: I couldn't have written to him as 'Mon cher Igor'. I could not write 'Mon cher Maître', he would have thought my wits had gone astray. I'd say to him, 'Bonjour, mon cher Igor', but in writing to him, I couldn't. It would have seemed familiar to me, it would have seemed petty. For me it was an ideal name, as Valéry was an ideal name, as Plato is an ideal name. I find them very close to one another, very alike in their approach to the essentials.

All great creators respect what is well made. With Ravel, for example, the making of the mechanism, the game with the material, was all part of the work. I knew Ravel . . . well, and not at all. We had very good relations, but the link which creates real communication was unfortunately never established. To tell the truth, a Ravel exists whom no one knew. He is Ravel, and even Ravel doesn't know who Ravel is. What matters to him is good craftsmanship in all circumstances, because devising a work is a mental game. Perhaps it's just a game in the consciousness of the writer, and only takes musical shape from the force of his personality, whether he's being frivolous or serious.

Your personal acquaintance with the man then, contributes nothing to your knowledge of the work?

It contributes everything on day-to-day occasions, but an artist's life is his work. The effect of the man Stravinsky on the artist Stravinsky is of little consequence.

That's essentially what he said himself during an interview, when he was asked to explain his technique. He tried to stammer out something but ended up saying. 'My nose is. My technique is.' So , no comment.

He was convinced that someone who didn't know how to take advantage of a wrong note wasn't a composer. That reminded me of Yvonne Printemps's theatre debut. In her first part, opposite Sacha Guitry, she had to come on stage, adorable as she was, and say: 'Je naquis un dimanche' (I was born on a Sunday). Instead of that, very nervous and all at sea, she came on and gabbled, 'Je quinas un mandiche'! It was the hit of the evening! So it's do-mi-re instead of do-re-mi. It's the same thing.

During the 1930s, turning his back completely on the composer of The
Rite of Spring *and* Les Noces, *Stravinsky moved towards a sort of
neo-Classicism, even going in the direction of Weber, Bellini, or
Tchaikovsky. Then in the 1950s, he began to use serial technique. Many
people have seen this as a self-betrayal. Do you think there was a
definitive break?*

A man isn't made of one image but of a multitude. It is the
composition of images that make up the man.

Some thought that there was a break in Stravinsky's career. I
think rather that he sought to appease a new hunger. His evolution
was great but everything he sampled belonged to him.

Take Beethoven's first Sonata: doh, fa, la, doh, fa, la, . . . All
the tragedy leading us to the Ninth Symphony is there. Take the
second Sonata: la, mi, mi, re, doh, si, la — and all of a sudden you
have *commedia dell'arte*. It's the same Beethoven, who looks now
left, now right.

Stravinsky had that skill. He saw. One day we were on the
terrace of a restaurant in Venice, when a flock of seagulls
suddenly flew past. He said, 'One had a broken claw.' I'd seen
nothing, whereas he spent his time seeing.

He wasn't a stranger anywhere. There wasn't one Stravinsky
in Paris, another Stravinsky in New York, another in Los
Angeles. There was a single Stravinsky who could assimilate
Paris, New York, Helsinki, Poland, the whole world, the moon,
and remain Stravinsky.

You could apply to him Cocteau's saying, 'An original artist
cannot copy: he has only to copy to be original.'

Stravinsky evolved his language without losing any of his
personality. He relied on the given, which could be Bach,
Tchaikovsky or Gesualdo, it didn't matter. One day, he decided
to write a work on themes by Pergolesi. Are there any two more
different artists in the world? How could such a singular mish-
mash produce a work?

The result was *Pulcinella*, a masterpiece in which Pergolesi
remains a hundred per cent Pergolesi, and Stravinsky a hundred
per cent Stravinsky, and the unity of the piece emerges from their
differences. Even if Stravinsky writes 'in the manner of' it
remains Stravinsky, the signature is there. His personality is so
peremptory that, when he picks up something, you don't see the
object so much as the hand holding it.

He was inspired by a work, a technique, a manner of being, and
then altered everything. And each time people said: 'What a pity

With Igor Stravinsky

Mr Stravinsky has lost his true path!' He would reply, 'These people are extraordinary. They condemn my latest works without perceiving that there, in a single movement, there is more music than in all the previous works.'

Many of Stravinsky's works are still not known by young musicians or to the public. *Petrushka* goes like a letter in the post — assuming the post is functioning properly. But *Threni*, the *Cantatas* or the *Requiem Canticles* are very rarely played. Still, the continuity is plain.

Luther said of Josquin des Prés, 'He is the master of his notes.'

Similarly, Stravinsky is the master of his means of composition, even if he borrows them from his neighbours; all is well with him from the moment he finds productive material, a subject to build on. In the work of any great composer you always find certain hallmarks; these are probably the involuntary traits of the person expressing them. What I'm saying is a bit confused because it's muddled in my mind and reaches further than I can go.

But Stravinsky's writing is very striking in this way. In a manuscript score of two hundred pages, there is not one bar-line less well-drawn than another, not a clef that is less beautiful than another! One day at his house in Hollywood, catching sight of a page of the final version of *Danse Sacrale* on his desk, I couldn't help exclaiming: 'What a copy! How splendid!' He said to me: 'I must start over again.'

'You want to change something?'

'No, touch it.'

'I don't touch manuscripts, I look at them.'

'Touch it all the same.'

Somewhere he'd made a correction, scratching it out, and the paper was slightly spoilt. He'd recopied the whole page. He'd never asked himself, 'What do I care?'

It's very instructive to have access to his manuscripts, it makes you aware that this is a man in full control. The fact that he's a volcano devoured by all sorts of passions doesn't diminish the rigour at all.

I have here the flyleaf of the manuscript of the *Symphony of Psalms*, which, he assured me, had cost him more work than copying out the whole score. He had to find a way of saying that the work was dedicated to the Boston Symphony Orchestra, but that it had been written to the glory of God. You do not write a *Symphony of Psalms* for the Boston Symphony, you give them the occasion to play it; the two are not to be confused.

A pause for curiosity

I returned to Budapest one day knowing that Zoltan Kodaly had remarried. I had known the first Madame Kodaly well, she had been twenty years older than he and exceptionally intelligent. And I said to myself: 'I will go back to the house, but Emma will have disappeared.'

On my arrival, Kodaly greeted me with the words: 'I am lucky to have seven children around me, but Emma remains queen of the house.' It was rather painful, they still laid a place for her at the table where we all had lunch.

At ninety-seven, ill, knowing that she was going to die, she occupied herself with working out who her husband should marry, because there was no question of his remaining alone. She herself made the selection from the possible candidates: 'That one, no, I don't think so, she's a bit egotistical. That one . . . not her either. The other . . . Impossible!' Finally she set her heart on a little orphan in whom they had both taken an interest, and said, 'Oh her, I like her a lot.' That was all. When she died, Kodaly was eighty, he married the little girl of twenty. There was no feeling of betrayal, or of usurping her place: a woman of ninety-seven had died; she had been replaced by a girl of twenty.

In the same way, I perfectly understand that Madame Casals might remarry. She was still very young when Casals died, he had married her when over eighty and she was a marvellous wife to him.

I'm not very up to date, nor in fact very interested in such things, but from time to time, as now, I have a flicker of curiosity, quite deceptive however, because you generally misinterpret what happens to people. The marriage that seems oddest to me, though, is Jacqueline Kennedy's to Onassis. It seems curious to say the least. Too many millions into the bargain!

The Princess de Polignac

A little while after his Paris debut, Yehudi Menuhin played three concertos at the Opera, three masterpieces: Bach, Brahms, Beethoven. And who was playing with such mastery, such understanding, such gravity, such warmth, such purity, three of the most significant concertos in the repertoire? A little boy of eleven, blond, clear-eyed, still childlike. The audience's growing enthusiasm passed from murmurs of satisfaction to astonishment, to extraordinary emotion in fact.

It was no longer a matter of hearing a virtuoso, but of listening to the works in all their integrity. Every condition was satisfied: the music, liberated, was sovereign.

Coming out of the concert, overwhelmed, I cannot express to what degree, I met two of my pupils and . . . Manuel de Falla, whom I asked to come and spend a few minutes with us at the Café de la Paix, so that I could introduce my pupils, who dreamed of making his acquaintance.

'I can't, I'm ill, I promised my sister that I'd go and lie down.'

'Look, tell your sister I'll take responsibility. Ten minutes won't change your health. Come for ten minutes.'

He came. His conversation was dazzling and charmed my two pupils, whose combined ages didn't add up to his. Then he returned to Menuhin's concert, 'Yes, yes, it overwhelms me, a child prodigy. But what shatters me even more is an elderly prodigy. Verdi writing *Falstaff* at eighty astounds me more than Mozart writing his masterpieces at twenty.'

I can still hear that voice, so timid and so assured, because whatever his timidity or reserve, his words represented certainty.

He was often to be seen in Paris. I greatly admired him and knew him quite well, without being so close to him as to know exactly how much time he spent in Paris and when he returned to Spain for good. From his house in Grenada there was a magnificent view, for miles and miles; but the house itself wasn't luxurious, in fact quite modest, almost an image of poverty, of sobriety, of asceticism corresponding to his inner life.

I know of a photograph of Falla, in which his head reminds you of a Benedictine monk from the Middle Ages; an extraordinary photograph with that particular shape of the head, sculptural and severe, reflecting in a striking way the spiritual atmosphere of his music. But all that is fortuitous. I've never liked that kind of association and think that you shouldn't try to link what you weigh with the thoughts you carry around. That's another thing altogether.

He had been commissioned by the Polignacs for an important work. . .

Yes, *Master Peter's Puppet Show.*

Princess de Polignac's salon was one of the centres of artistic and musical life in Paris between the wars. Princess Edmond was American and adored the arts. The birthday present she wanted as a girl of fifteen was a performance of a Beethoven quartet. Her collection of paintings was fabulous, and it was while arguing over the purchase of a painting that she met the man who was to become her husband, Prince Edmond de Polignac. It was even said that he finally decided to marry her in order to gain Monet's *Turkeys*, which was part of his future wife's collection. She must have been at least thirty and he twice her age. As he himself was the son of elderly parents, she claimed that her father-in-law was born under Louis XV.

With Marie-Blanche de Polignac and Maria Modrakowska

Living in Paris, London or Venice, passionate about music, she had made the pilgrimage to Bayreuth in company with Chabrier and Fauré, and became one of the last great patrons in history.

Everywhere she went, Greek was translated, Latin was translated, music was made. She'd arrive in London and an hour later, you'd be playing music or reading poems. How many *soirées* we all went to or helped with, where we played lots of Monteverdi, Schutz's *Resurrection,* Carissimi's *Jephte,* and then all the works she commissioned!

Much ill was said of her; but I only know her great generosity; she was not blind — she would discriminate. And with discrimination, she gave a great deal and is owed a great deal. There was the famous evening when her butler entered, appalled, 'Madame la Princesse, four pianos have arrived . . .'. Stravinsky's *Les Noces* was to be played for the first time. She was really interested in beauty and the production of beauty. Thus she naturally commissioned works. She was creative. She would hear someone talked about, she would summon him; she would hear talk of a work; she would listen to it, she would commission.

It was thus that she first of all put in an order for Fauré's songs called 'From Venice'. Then there was *Puppet Show* from Falla, *Les Noces* from Stravinsky, *Le Diable Boiteux* from Jean Françaix and Markevitch's *Cantata*. At that time, Jean Françaix and Igor Markevitch were completely unknown.

And was it through you that she made their acquaintance?

I don't know whether it was through me. She wasn't easily influenced. She used to say, 'I shall see.' And she would see. And if it didn't please her, she wouldn't see.

Naturally she was marked by her time as Diaghilev was marked by his, as Liszt, that genius, that giant, had been marked by his time, and had played an essential role in the creation of contemporary works.

All these scores were later performed for her, in the great drawing-room of her mansion on the Avenue Georges Mandel, which today is the Hôtel de la Fondation Singer-Polignac. For she left her fortune to the Collège de France, and the Collège de France collects the annuities from her bequest, which allows them to keep hospitals going, or to continue supporting artists and scholars who never knew that she was helping them and who continue to receive an allowance. All this was done in secret.

Wasn't it in the Polignac salon that you took part in the rediscovery of Monteverdi, then totally forgotten; conducting and performing his madrigals and operas for the first time in centuries?

Let's not exaggerate. I would very much like to have rediscovered Monteverdi single-handedly, but unfortunately that wasn't the case. As a child, I was somewhat on the fringe because, wanting to escape what was conventional, I tried to discover things. I hope I've inspired my pupils with this need to discover and invent, not to destroy but to augment. As far as Monteverdi is concerned, Vincent d'Indy and Charles Bordes had done the preparatory work for a remarkable edition, but with one fault: they translated it into French. Now, Monteverdi cannot be sung in French, any more than Purcell or *Boris Godunov*. So we owe the very great edition of a very great composer to Malipiero.

Let's say that Monteverdi's works were simply not played and you were the first to record them.

It was the result of a happy chance. My vocal group played lots of music and I profited from exceptional performers. Irène Kedroff, Marie-Blanche de Polignac, Nathalie Kedroff, Paul Derenne, Hughes Cuenod, and Doda Conrad. I had nothing to do with their voices blending in such an astonishing way. Did I have the idea of making a record of Monteverdi? Or was it Princess Edmond, who was looking out for new things? You are asking more than I can now remember. It was in the air at the time. Monteverdi awaited his day, and his day came.

Talents and Explanations

Interpretation

I have always preferred the word 'transmit' to 'interpret', it seems to take better account of the attitude necessary to those whose job it is to shed light on a work. There was a period when anything was allowed, when the work was abandoned to the vandalism of interpreters. In my opinion, once the interpreter takes over, the game becomes unbalanced. The interpreter gains, but the work loses. A sublime interpretation is essentially one which makes me forget the composer, forget the interpreter, forget myself; I forget everything except the masterpiece. When I stand before the portrait of Titus in the National Gallery in London, I don't see it if it's badly lit, but it's there. It only has to be properly lit for me to see it.

I believe that a work of art transcends all its interpreters.

Don't you think that reduces the role of the interpreter, which shouldn't consist of merely illuminating a work, but even more of putting it in a new, unexpected, unsuspected light?

On the contrary, I think it's the highest praise to say that the supreme interpreter becomes invisible. The interpreter has to be exceptional if he is to submerge himself utterly in the work, identifying himself with it rather than it with himself, though he inevitably does that to some extent. But I believe he must think only of the work.

Still, you always recognize the signature of a great interpretation.

It's dreadful, but honestly I must say that I forget, I hear nothing but the work. One day Cortot confided to me:
'Do you know, you once said something that has touched me

more than anything else? It was twenty years ago, I had just played Chopin's *Preludes* and you came . . .'

'Ah! I remember,' I interrupted him.

After a concert in which he had played the *Preludes,* I'd been to see him in his dressing-room and declared, 'A lot of people are asking me for my opinion, to describe how you played. I have no idea. All I know is that I've never found the *Preludes* so beautiful.'

He had focused all his light on the *Preludes,* not the other way round. I had heard the work in all its splendour. My forgetting the interpreter wasn't neglect, on the contrary. It put him very high, because the light of someone who is nothing illuminates nothing.

Don't you think that someone who plays the same piece hundreds of times, night after night, concert after concert, will eventually be tired of it?

There's a more tragic example: the priest who has lost his faith. What is his duty? I have not had a religious vocation, I have not been a priest, I have not lost my faith. Thus I am not qualified to judge, but I can imagine it. I think that I would endeavour to keep up appearances with regard to others. I might play the Kreutzer Sonata, though I had lost my faith in it, but I would know how it should be played.

Must the priest confess openly that he has lost faith? I would say no, because it might lead to doubt in those people too weak to defend themselves. In my opinion it would come down to a sacrifice of the real power of his role as priest, for personal motives.

You might then ask whether that interpretation of the Kreutzer Sonata is going to be as convincing, whether the priest would be fulfilling his functions to the same extent, after losing his faith.

If he is a great man, so much the better! You have to keep your head above water in order to swim. 'The letter killeth, the spirit giveth life.' You say: 'In the name of the Father and of the Son, and of the Holy Ghost, Amen.' After having said those words many times throughout your life, you might go into a church one day and make the sign of the cross without thinking of anything. That day, you are marked by the sign but are indifferent to it.

That happens to everyone, but it doesn't mean your faith is extinguished forever.

Let's transpose that to the realm of art. Could art be above all the art of illusion?

And why not? Isn't what you call illusion close to reality?

Once there was a performance of *Horace*, at the Forum in Rome. And when the procession arrived with the litter bearing Camille, suddenly there was a full moon, a marvellous full moon; midnight began to chime. It wasn't planned in the production. The whole procession stood motionless until the twelfth stroke. The dramatic effect was extraordinary. Twelve strokes: boom, boom, boom . . . When you know the setting, the two columns, the full moon, the entire history, we are taken back centuries.

You attended this performance?

Someone told me about it. But in a sense I was there because I can see it. It would be dishonest to say that I wasn't there. I'm inventing it — and I'm not.

An incident: I'm four, it's Christmas time. We have a neighbour on the first floor. Mother says to me: 'Go and say Merry Christmas to Madame Delpuget.' I arrive at Madame Delpuget's, she says, 'How nice of you to come. Tell me, have you had a good Christmas? What have you been given?'

'A teddy-bear, a — I don't know what — a farm!'

She, rather hysterical, exclaims, 'A farm? A real farm?' At that moment, I see the farm, and I begin to describe to her the farm I see. The next day Mother says to me, 'What got into you? What did you tell Madame Delpuget?'

'Just about my farm.

And Mother who was never wrong, made a mistake here. She punished me for having lied. Eighty-five years have gone by and I still see that farm of mine, describing it to Madame Delpuget on the first floor, 30 rue La Bruyère! I see it all. I picture to myself a very old lady. In fact, she probably wasn't so old. She was perhaps forty, but she gave me the impression she was two hundred! Her stupefaction, 'A farm! A real farm!', and my saying, 'Yes, a real farm, with the house, animals, sheep, cattle.' It grew into a Versailles!

Well, to return to your question about art and illusion, I would say, the art of reality, of a transposed reality. The work is stronger than its audience.

If I play *Tristan*, I don't think of Wagner, nor that Furtwängler is conducting. I think of *Tristan*. The interpreter forgets himself. His personality only enters into it unconsciously, transposed. I don't

use a work of art to make believe that I am Tristan and Isolde. If I
long to be Tristan and Isolde, it would be better to have some nice
little affaire, which undoubtedly would be less sensational than
theirs; but I cannot use Tristan and Isolde in the belief that I too
am acting out a grand passion and that I shall die of it! There is
Tristan and Isolde and then me, precious little, at the receiving
end; I understand or don't understand. When I listen to music I
should like to be able to disappear entirely.

Nadia Boulanger in concert

Interpreters

BUSONI

Ferrucio Busoni was a genius. To say that he played the piano in an extraordinary way is merely to state the blindingly obvious.

I recall a concert when he played Liszt's 'The Legend of St Francis of Assisi Preaching to the Birds' in a way that revealed the greatest depths in the work; listening to it, I tried to pin down what he did that made it seem so extraordinary. It wasn't until I had heard it three times that I realized he had managed the incredible *tour de force* of giving to the trills scattered all over the page the same number of notes — but this kind of feat didn't matter. Above all, you sensed a unity in his interpretations. But on the other hand, he was a demon for invention; was he as great a creator as he was a genius himself? I leave the question open.

He was not greater than Beethoven. He was not greater than Mozart. He was among the greatest. He played in a singular way, with the air of composing as he played; and I think that his achievement would have been greater if he had not tried to make Mozart say what he, Busoni, saw in him — which he liked to add.

Hence the necessity for watchdogs in matters of interpretation. In any event, Busoni's articulation was perfect, and came not only from the astonishing evenness of his technique, but above all from his prodigious sense of rhythm.

One mistake that should never be made is tampering with the tempo. What gives a piece of music its unity, its essential character, its dominant character? It is the underlying pulse, which must be respected even when other liberties are taken and one uses what is called 'rubato'. The rubato of a really serious musician doesn't break the unity of the beat. Take a record by Toscanini, put on your metronome and you will see that everything is in marvellous accord. Liberty can only exist within the scope of a regular, severe, immutable pulse.

YSAYE AND PUGNO

Nevertheless the period which you knew well — between the wars — seems to me to have been marked by a style of interpretation that took curious liberties with rhythm.

I'm not so sure, and in any case that wasn't so with the very great, neither Casals nor Toscanini nor Kreisler, nor anyone important.

You are taking a period which, in chamber music, was extraordinarily rich. The Busch Quartet in Germany, the Capet Quartet in France were playing splendidly then, and at about the same time, or a bit before, there were — each separately having made great careers — Raoul Pugno and Eugene Ysaye, that tremendous, astounding violinist.

I participated in their rehearsals, and one day when Ysaye was in the midst of working in short stages on the Franck Sonata — it was at a time when I dared sight-read no matter what in front of no matter whom, like the poor fool I was — I said to him, 'But why are you working so hard on this Sonata?' He became very serious: 'Do you realize that we play this more than a hundred times a year? If it wasn't worked on, it would be intolerable!'

He played it with Pugno?

Almost always with Pugno. They were two interpreters made for playing together, those two giants.

Pugno is someone who has practically disappeared from people's memories.

Like many of the interpreters from that period. And I haven't mentioned Weingartner, Nikisch, all those tremendous ones; even Toscanini is probably already a bit far away for you; they go so fast.

But Pugno was also a composer. Didn't you collaborate on an opera with him?

Yes, and some songs. Because of that my sister and I were put in touch with Verhaeren and with Gabriele d'Annunzio. We had quite close dealings with them: d'Annunzio, deep down, was intimidated; this audacious, reckless man was timid with my sister because a young girl — she was just a girl then — represented a human type that he didn't often have occasion to meet, and that made a great impression on him. It was the same

Nadia Boulanger and Raoul Pugno

with Maeterlinck, who had been extraordinarily touching when my sister asked permission to set *La Princesse Maleine* to music. She died without having time to compose more than fragments, very important ones but fragments all the same. Not being a composer, I couldn't comply with her wish and my duty, which would have been to assemble and finish them.

But as regards performers, I remember very little that I can express in precise terms. I hear pieces, I hear sonorities and sometimes I don't even remember the name of the interpreter any more. It must be said that I don't like being aware of the actor who is playing Hamlet; in seeing Hamlet, I'd like to forget the actor and even Shakespeare himself. It is the spirit that must be encountered. And yet, I'll tell you something amazing! You know my mania for turning on the radio at the drop of a hat; recently I heard something marvellous and said to myself, 'Really, you'd swear that is Kathleen Ferrier . . . my blind, profound, tested, heartfelt admiration . . . I don't know, all the same there's no one else who sings like her!' Well, it was her! It happened to be a recording she made with Barbirolli just before her death. This dying woman's voice was absolutely intact; her records are simply overwhelming.

One day, after a recital she gave at the Champs Elysées Theatre, I had invited her to dinner; and as we were going out the dining-room door, I said to her: 'I hope that one day we will be able to make music together.' In a strange voice she said to me 'Oh! music. . .'. I thought she preferred not to commit herself to singing with me, and said nothing more. But she knew that she had sung for one of the last times. Thirty two years old. . .

FRANCIS PLANTÉ

Francis Planté was a great French pianist. He'd been an amazing child prodigy. When he was eight, he went to play one evening at Liszt's. In the brilliant salon were Liszt in his abbé's robe, and then all the duchesses, grand-duchesses, super-duchesses, everyone. The little boy played, Liszt played, after which they rose for supper. A gentleman went up to little Francis and said to him: 'You see that gentleman all by himself in the corner; go and ask him to play for you, he'll come.' The boy said, 'Sir, would you come and play for me?' The gentleman sat down to play. Who was the gentleman in question? Chopin. That took place between little Francis Planté and Chopin all alone. Those who went into the dining-room didn't even hear the music.

Did Francis Planté tell you this?

He told me, when he used to stay at the Hotel des Saints-Pères, rue des Saints-Pères, where he used to receive you as they say Glenn Gould does — in an unbelievable muddle with clothes hung up in the middle of the room. He was most original and very intelligent. The young people who used to spend the summer working at Mont-de-Marsan, where Planté was their host, would return worn out. You would say to them:
'What's up with you? You look ill.'
'But I've come from Francis Planté's.'
'And so?'
'Oh well, you know, you get up at 6 a.m. to go hunting, return to work, then have lunch, then coffee, play music; then you play cards, and to finish you do some sight-reading. Morning till night, not a moment's rest.'

Such were the days from which boys of twenty-two or twenty-three returned dead by the end of a month. Planté himself, at eighty or more, was as fresh as a rose! Like Rubinstein today.

Rubinstein doesn't want to impress anyone. We have known each other since . . . I can't even count how many years. He tells stories over lunch in such an irresistible way that I can hardly eat for weeping with laughter.

POULENC

It was the same with Francis Poulenc. I can't remember without laughing one dinner with friends where he told us an absolutely uninteresting story. He had arrived at the Vienna railway station to board his sleeper; the sleeper was already occupied by somebody he had to turn out. A banal story. He told it to us so that we laughed until we cried, his description of the stunned expression of the rather dim carriage attendant, and of the man who had to be removed was so droll. This was not at all amusing in itself and yet it was irresistible; so was his way of playing his own work at the piano.

You'd never have heard Poulenc play *Les Mamelles de Tiresias?* It was dazzling, fireworks. He played with too much pedal, it was drowned, but it rang out in an unforgettable way.

Francis Poulenc's personality was much more complex than met the eye. He was entirely paradoxical. You could meet him as easily in fashionable Parisian circles as at the Vierge de Rocamadour [a place of pilgrimage] or at Mass. He was very religious, and I hardly feel qualified to size him up.

I have a letter in which he writes (I'm not quoting precisely): 'A shabby critic has accused me of being just as interested in a soldier in the Bois de Vincennes as in vital matters of the day. Unfortunately it's true. I take these different aspirations into account, having received from my family on the one hand a Parisian heritage, on the other the cloister; I follow them both.' And it's true that side by side in his work are pieces with flashes of very light humour, and pages of deep religious feeling

You mentioned the irresistible manner in which Poulenc, the pianist, interpreted his works. You also said how Markevitch, the composer, gave up composing to devote himself to conducting. Don't you find it curious that a whole series of musicians — interpreters and composers both — almost always lean in one direction or the other? I'm thinking of Enesco in particular.

left to right: Jean Françaix, Pierre Bernac, Francis Poulenc,
Nadia Boulanger,Maurice Gendron at Fontainebleau

For Enesco it was cruel, because he pursued head-on his two activities of violinist and composer. Since he was adored as a violinist he was frustrated in his life as a composer. Deep down, only composing mattered to him. I think no one met Enesco without revering him; he was a very great person, totally disinterested.

When you went to a concert where Menuhin and Enesco were playing, there was Enesco, dazzled by Menuhin, and Menuhin primarily concerned to let Enesco go in front of him, showing, even on stage, his reverence and devotion. It was very moving. Enesco was a person of such great stature, such great significance. For all of us he remained an emblem of generosity, of profound musical knowledge, in his innermost soul.

In your opinion, what work of his will last?

I don't think he has exercised the influence that he should have as a composer. It's a great pity, because like Bartok, he knew how to speak the true language of his native land. I don't mean this in the popular sense, but more profoundly: he succeeded in expressing in his music the very soul of his people. Well, time will tell.

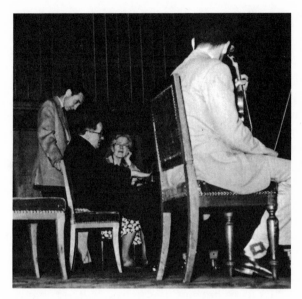

With Georges Enesco at Fontainebleau

Leaving aside the ages and cultures in which the distinction between the functions of composer and interpreter isn't made, that division of labour generally accepted these days, do you think a great composer can be an equally great interpreter?

You only need to have heard Debussy play once. I don't mean that he played better than others. He played otherwise, he had his own tone, his unique tone.

Was that also true of Ravel?

No. He did play, but the tone wasn't compelling. He was awkward at the piano. As for Stravinsky, he didn't have the dexterity of a great pianist, but he could never be awkward; when he played the beginning of *Capriccio,* you'd have it in your head for ever. You'd never hear it again like that. And if you want to know what a real Stravinsky rhythm is, you must listen to it as he conducts it.

That is the reason why he preferred to record his works rather than provide a commentary on them. On paper, he indicated the notes to be played. In recording them, he gives us his instructions, he shows us the direction to take.

Change and Permanence

In a letter to Reynaldo Hahn, Proust writes: 'At every moment of our life we are the descendants of ourselves, and the atavism which weighs on us is our past, preserved by habit.'

That seems to me profoundly true; I am not five, ten or sixty years old, and I'm not eighty; I am all of them at once. And what happens today illuminates what I felt unconsciously at five or six.

But what failures in between! It is only in the context of convent or cloister that I might have had some chance of seeing through successfully what I would have hoped to accomplish. I didn't have the strength for that, and I wasn't attracted by the cloistered life. My existence, confined enough within its own rule, in a sense was not so different, but without my ever having had the privilege of devoting it to the essential, and arranging the rest accordingly.

The essential for you being music; you have been enclosed in music?

Yes, but I'm well aware that music, without the ingredient which derives from its transcendent meaning, doesn't exist. It is in the name of what is beyond, of what dominates the whole situation, that I live in music.

I'm very troubled by the phenomenon of fashion. Today, Mozart is ranked much higher than he was when I was a child. Later there was a fashion for Mozart, but it wasn't that which made Mozart one of those spirits who enrich the world, a world containing treasures that span the ages. There is also ephemeral fashion, what it's good form to admire. That doesn't affect me.

Since I'm an old fusspot, I don't much like change; change impelled by inner necessity is fine, change because one doesn't know where to go is fatal and destructive.

But you do not stand aloof from your times. I noticed that the latest work by Xenakis is on the programme for your analysis course at Fontainebleau.

Yes of course, it's not a discovery.

No, I merely wanted to say that he's a contemporary, fully active composer and that you don't ignore his work.

That would be unfortunate. If I were to list all the composers I like — or that I don't so much like as respect — there would be a good many. But don't imagine that I'm about to give out prizes. I wouldn't allow myself to, because I don't feel qualified to do so. I keep abreast of things, that's all.

Today I know time is limited — there are so many things I love, I revere, I return to — I also know that I can't add on endlessly. It's impossible. There needs to be time for assimilation, time for remembering. Even now I marvel how a piece can be played that I've known for eighty years, which still sounds new to me. I re-read Plato's dialogues, they're new; I re-read *Hamlet*, that's new! And there is all the rest to understand, that I still haven't understood. He who comes to it in ten years, twenty, fifty, will find *Hamlet* ever more rich, more charged with thought, imagination, painful reality.

You see many people chasing after discovery instead of delving deeper; that becomes the exercise. At all costs an unknown masterpiece must be found. Such things exist, no doubt, but they are fewer than masterpieces that are simply under-rated. At present there is a whole set of people so afraid of missing an unknown masterpiece that they take up everything; the less they understand, the more enthusiastic they are. Recently I heard a piece that made me wonder whether the composer was ill, drugged, or in the grip of a serious mental obsession. There are certainly works that are taken for grave mental aberrations at the time of their creation, and which are masterpieces, but I don't believe that happens more than once a century. Also it's necessary to allow time to see things individually.

Can you imagine my panic when I visited the Hermitage in Leningrad! I had an hour to spend there. I had to see everything! It was a question of honour for the curators. We began rushing from one room to another, into a third, a fourth. To be honest, I really saw nothing. Whereas I stayed an hour in front of one column on the Acropolis, and it was there I had a feeling of discovery. But at the Hermitage the curators believed they were offering me every pleasure, while I only had an impression of speed, the distress of going so fast, and missing everything. However that may be, the fact of ceaselessly returning to what constitute the treasures of existence should not prevent anyone from giving attention to what there is today, to what will be tomorrow.

Suddenly you become aware of a new perspective that seems to cloud over the previous perspective. But all things considered, is the music of Ravel, of Xenakis, of Boulez or whoever you think important, so distant from that of Guillaume de Machaut? In the end you can put an old-master drawing beside a drawing by

Picasso, and they are charmed to make each other's acquaintance.

You have witnessed what has happened in twentieth-century music. In your youth, you knew what were still considered the 'audacities' of Gounod, whose audaciousness obviously rather escapes us; you knew Stravinsky and practically all the people who counted in the musical world of the twentieth century. How would you define the main trends or the main trend, if there is one, of music in this century?

The answer is easy because there are some big dates, some points of reference; you can enumerate a certain number of works. Even limiting yourself to five or six, you have *Pelléas, Les Noces* — whether you like them or not — you have *Wozzeck, Bluebeard's Castle*, the *Symphony of Psalms*. You have works that answer to the times.

You don't have any sense of a break?

Of change, I don't like the word 'break'.

From the strictly technical point of view, don't you think that Schönberg, for example, introduced a certain radical departure in ways of thinking about music?

Do you think this will seem such a great split in fifty years? In the history of the world, fifty years is a minute! When *Pelléas* was performed for the first time, people imagined when they heard the orchestra tuning up that it was *Pelléas*. And when we began playing Monteverdi's music again, it was thought to be dreadful. And when my dear father was writing his charming *opéras-comique*, very well written but in the pure French tradition of *opéra-comique*, he was reproached, as I've told you, with having given himself over to German techniques. What does it mean?

There are such prejudices, there's a dreadful danger of habit; now habits are not traditions. I think people realize that today. Debussy has already gone through his purgatory. Fauré is still in the shade because he's one of those who never had a very large audience, but it is very striking to see that all today's young people realize that this supreme distinction, this supreme sobriety, this true classicism, is very important.

Do you think it's possible, no matter what the period, to establish a hierarchy among composers?

It seems to me very difficult to award degrees. 'You're number one, and he, number three or seven. . .'. I find that difficult.

Still, you must think that the work of a Beethoven is more important than the work of a Max Bruch, for example. . .

You are getting into deep waters there! You're saying: the Himalayas or the Butte Montmartre! It's difficult for me to compare the Butte Montmartre with the Himalayas, but in the end, I must honestly say that I hardly think of Max Bruch at all, whereas I've rarely spent a day without thinking of Beethoven. In a fit of bad temper you could be anti-Beethoven one day; against, but never indifferent.

And yet, isn't there a hierarchy among the so-called avant-garde composers and those who retrace their own steps, even though critics are still uneasy about establishing precise criteria?

You never retrace steps; or rather, it is the situation of Lot's wife. Once she turns around, she's changed into a pillar of salt.

You can lean on yesterday to construct tomorrow, but you cannot build tomorrow by starting all over again what was done yesterday.

You think then that everything is evolution and nothing is a break?

Yes, I'd tend to think so, but the answer should be categorical. You can't be categorical because when you've lived for a long time you don't even understand how you have been able to adapt to such different ways of life, imperceptibly. You know, many people tell me, out of kindness or politeness: 'You don't change'. I know what is there. What is it clinging to? Something inside me is really worn out, has run down, but the seams are just about holding.

You play Stravinsky's *Capriccio* and at the end you know it's in G. Is it the same thing as a symphony by Haydn? No, but there are a lot of points in common. Each successive stage brings something new which has its own value, but there is no genius without ancestors.

You often discover a tacit, unbroken link between generations, which makes them converge. In the Archduke Trio there are bars which seem to derive directly from Fauré. One E natural in the key of B flat major, which probably occurs quite by chance in Beethoven, is so characteristic of Fauré that when you hear it, you say to yourself: 'But it's incredible, that's Fauré already.' Beethoven certainly didn't say to himself that he had written something new. And all those great diminished seventh chords in Scarlatti, that's already Beethoven! One day a man like Dutilleux appears on the scene, whose personality is very marked. But there again, how would you define it? He only used seven notes like everyone else, and even if he used quarter-tones and demi-quarter tones, it would have been the same.

The language is common, but each person is unique and either has powers of invention or doesn't. We're told that two and two make four. But if the mind is imaginative and finds that two and two make something else, at that moment something else happens — something troublesome, because it sometimes produces results. An imaginative person has an option on the unknown.

The day that Mr Richard Wagner decided to write *The Ring*, he took a stroll into the unknown; eighteen hours of music which holds together, it's incredible.

The difference lies in the perception of an individual thought, which must combine with a universal thought. That belongs to a concept of the cosmos we are trying to visualize. This is rather vague but it is what I sense. A method can be either entirely good or entirely bad and it's all the same to me whether you write one way or another.

The appearance of polyphony, following on plain-chant, represented a major event in the evolution of music, but it didn't destroy what existed. All things have their times of eclipse: the sun must rise and set.

Don't you think that the intellectual processes of a Schönberg, deliberately working out a radically new and restrictive system, consisted in raising a barrier against the disorder which he felt was being established, or that he himself was creating?

You're talking theology to me; it's an area where I'm afraid my ignorance prevents me from following you. I cannot step back and look at it.

There are periods in which the concern with music or art is intellectual, explicatory, and others that give more elbow-room to freedom. Conventions are the points of reference that give a certain form to evolution, and when there has been a long spell of intellectual order, a swing towards intuitive order follows. But if there isn't any intellectual order in the intuitive order or no intuitive in the intellectual, then something is missing. This year I received a letter which went thus: 'Mademoiselle, the cow is better, my wife is dead, the trees are shooting up. My respects.' Well, that's a very real letter. Some would find it improper to talk so crudely and simultaneously of the death of a wife and the healing of a cow. The author of this letter doesn't confuse his cow

Doda Conrad

1935: that year, I met Mademoiselle Boulanger. I auditioned for
her and she offered me a place in her newly formed vocal
ensemble. I already had a well-established reputation as a lieder
singer, but the privilege of making music with Nadia Boulanger
was worth the occasional sacrifice of my international career
demands.

In those days her concert activity was very limited, mostly to
programmes of unusual music to illustrate her lectures on music
history at the Ecole Normale de Musique, or at Fontainebleau.
Every winter she would organize several afternoon recitals at the
'Cercle Interallié', and on occasion she conducted concerts of
vocal and instrumental music in the mansion of Princess Edmond
de Polignac.

Nadia Boulanger had endeavoured to form an ideally balanced
vocal ensemble. From Switzerland she brought the angelic
voiced, high soprano Gisèle Peyron, and the counter tenor
Hugues Cuenod; as a contrast, Russian-born Irène Kedroff —
mezzo-soprano — and contralto Nathalie Kedroff provided the
Slavic timbre; Marie-Blanche de Polignac, an outstanding
musician blessed with an adorable voice and faultless diction,
and *tenor de charme*, Paul Derenne, were French; Doda Conrad,
bass, is of Polish origin. All the singers were multi-lingual and
exceptional sight-readers. By 1937 the group had become a well-
trained, homogeneous ensemble. The repertoire was wide and
eclectic, ranging from early Renaissance to contemporary composers, above all, Igor Stravinsky.

In the autumn of 1936 I was on tour in England, and had the
opportunity to suggest to the BBC that it should broadcast
Monteverdi, sung by our vocal ensemble. Monteverdi was little
known in those days, except to a handful of musicians. Nadia
Boulanger had revealed this great Italian master to me. I received
enthusiastic support from M.D. Calvocoressi, the Greek musi-
cologist; he was an adviser to Arthur Wynn, head of the chamber
music division of the BBC. Wynn was sympathetic, and urged me
to send in recordings by the ensemble.

On my return to Paris at Christmas, I discussed with Nadia
Boulanger the possibility of making records. I found her reluc-
tant. The very principle of recording was contrary to her beliefs

and convictions. 'The interpretation of music', she said, 'is and should remain a fleeting moment. What right have we, how do we dare, to freeze forever something that is supposed to be a precious, unique experience? Besides,' she added, 'I am confident, my dear Doda, that you will not find a recording company interested in listing Monteverdi in its catalogue. As you well know, our repertoire is the *chasse gardée* of a small élite!'

Her scepticism made me all the more eager to investigate the chances of our making some records. The previous year I had myself recorded Brahms's 'Vier ernste Gesänge' for His Master's Voice in Paris. I contacted Georges Truc, their artistic director, and invited him to our forthcoming concert at the 'Interallié'. He called me the day after the concert to say that the idea was excellent. 'I think we can definitely plan a five-record Monteverdi album, provided you can get us a guarantee for 250 subscriptions. Do you think that's possible?'

I sought the advice of the President of the 'Cercle Interallié', Prince de Beauvan-Craon. The Prince simply unhooked the receiver on his desk, and called the first four names I had mentioned as possible subscribers: the Princess de Polignac, of course, and her nephew, Count Jean de Polignac (husband of Marie-Blanche); also Madame René Dujarric de la Rivière, and Arthur Sacks, the American financier. The four agreed to subscribe fifty albums each, with the Prince subscribing the remaining fifty. Needless to say, the five subscribers never had to disburse any of their guarantees; the first Monteverdi recordings in history met — as we know — with a tremendous success! They were a revelation to the world of music in the 1930s.

To convince Nadia Boulanger was another matter . . . More or less reluctantly, she finally agreed 'to follow you, Doda, in this crazy adventure'. Those were her words. 'I am doing it only because you have gone to so much trouble to arrange *cette folie*. It will be your responsibility if we break our necks!'

HMV allotted a truly shabby expenses budget. The musicians got the lion's share. As I recall, the singers had to be content with a miserable ten dollars per side of a record. Thank God Nadia Boulanger did not insist on my renting a harpsichord! The recording sessions took place in February 1937, in the old studio on the rue Albert, Paris. The setting in itself was inspiring: most of the great artists of the golden age have recorded there. In addition, Marie-Blanche de Polignac had provided a case of champagne. It put everyone — including Nadia Boulanger and the sound engineers — in the right mood.

There had been rough moments in the rehearsals. The singers would often lose their tempers; I was nervous; Nadia was nervous — at times she threatened to cancel everything. Actually, she did not really believe in what she was doing. She was constantly worried about accurate timing: remember these were the days of 78 r.p.m. recordings, and a side could not exceed four minutes and thirty seconds! I also had to insist on meticulous planning of every recording session, something she kept ignoring. At one point she burst out: 'I refuse to stand in front of a microphone with you all singing hopelessly flat!' The madrigals in question had to be deleted from the list, thus we were nine minutes short. Something had to be done to replace the two sides.

After the rehearsal Nadia Boulanger took me aside. 'Take the score of *Il Ballo delle Ingrate*. Do whatever you wish with it, as long as you can find something acceptable to fill nine minutes. I trust you and Marie-Blanche! Myself, I have no time at all. Good luck.' That night we worked with Madame de Polignac, armed with scissors and stop-watch, to arrange a custom-made, balanced, and we hoped logical sequence of recitatives, instrumental interludes and short choral commentaries.

I spent the following day establishing the orchestral material with two of Mademoiselle's students. We were copying the parts while Nadia was busy teaching in her studio next door. She never came into the dining-room to see what we were doing! Thus she was confronted with a totally unfamiliar arrangement when she faced the musicians at the rehearsal. Fortunately, there were not too many mistakes. Marie-Blanche and myself actually sight-read our parts. 'This is pure genius, Doda!' cried Mademoiselle, a formula she would often use when she did not mean a word of what she was saying . . . Still, our improvised cutting of *Il Ballo* went down in history with the success of the recording, and remained in our repertoire for twenty years. At every performance Nadia Boulanger would stumble over some of our blunders in the arrangement, but she never got round to correcting them.

After this first experience, she was somewhat reconciled to recording. I think she was happy with the result, above all because of the impact of these first Monteverdi records on a tremendously enlarged public. Her first albums have never been deleted from the company's catalogue, in almost half a century!

The BBC offered Nadia Boulanger a contract for Monteverdi broadcasts in their 'Foundations of Music series', in the autumn of 1937. . . . It has been the pride of my life to have had the privilege, and the luck, of forwarding, as best I could, the development of her career as a conductor — one of the most moving facets of Nadia Boulanger's genius.

Hugues Cuenod

It is difficult to describe in a few words Nadia Boulanger's influence on a young man coming from abroad, already with proven classic training, but lacking that finish, that polish, above all that profound vision — the musical philosophy — which assiduous attendance at the rue Ballu alone could give him. You came away from the course aware that the music, and especially the way of teaching, had provided a wisdom and unexpected serenity which made it easier to face life's difficulties. And then there was the very original repertoire of the 'Boulangerie'! The great masters certainly: Bach, Mozart, Schubert, later Monteverdi and Debussy, Stravinsky, Fauré, but also the unknowns — for me — from the Middle Ages and the Renaissance, which made you understand where the great had gained their knowledge and inspiration.

Her severity, a touch of harshness on occasion, was soon wrapped up in tenderness and humour, and left no trace of ill-feeling, only a sense of the justice of her reproaches — more often kindly, pointing you in the right direction — and the awareness of contact with near-perfection in her attitude towards music and intellectual life. This exceptional woman lacked only Saint Cecilia's halo, which many of her pupils must have provided mentally.

In 1937, Gisèle Peyron and I had been auditioned in Boston by Serge Koussevitsky. He'd engaged us for a Boston Symphony concert, to be conducted by Nadia Boulanger the following year. However in 1938 Nadia decided to conduct Fauré's *Requiem*, in which there is no tenor solo part. Extremely disappointed, I was resigned to not participating in the concert when I saw myself announced in the programme. Nadia was going to telephone and correct the error when she remembered the two pages where the tenors in the choir sing alone. On the pretext that those in the Boston choir had too strong an American accent, she asked me to sing the two pages solo, thus salvaging my self-esteem and Koussevitsky's, who wouldn't know how many soloists figure in the *Requiem*. Nadia, with her benevolence and affection, had found a way out of disappointing me. Koussevitsky never suspected for a moment the little trick played on him.

Yehudi Menuhin

I first met Nadia Boulanger when I was studying in Paris at the age of eleven and, of course, like every young man for decades before and decades since, I lost my heart to her. This was in 1927. I remember either that year or the following sitting next to her at a grand dinner given for the Anciens Premier Prix of the Conservatoire and discussing with her the great C Major Fugue of Bach for solo violin.

She never changed: perhaps this is of all the comments the one which is most characteristic of her.

Her dedication to her sister, the composer Lili Boulanger who died tragically young; her resolve never to marry: her indefatigable pursuit of all that was most rigorous and beautiful in music and in terms of human behaviour; her strong and yet tender hand in guiding the young; the infinite trust which she inspired in all those who knew her; her commitment added to the fact that everyone knew where they would find her, what she would think and what standards she would uphold — these qualities together added up to a sense of security, a presence that combined the firmness and reliability of the Rock of Gibraltar with the loving solicitude of a mother.

Only once did I experience the intense anger that this extraordinary *grande dame* controlled so well. I remain amazed by her. It is true that the richness and breadth of her character were demanding, but it was refined by the powerful reality of a personality not the less flesh and blood for having unflinchingly obeyed the most rigorous principles of religion, as of music.

Nadia's contribution to my Music School will not be forgotten, both in the direct contact through music, her uncompromising demands on the children's concentration and self-discipline, and at the same time the inspiration she radiated. There is no one else I know who could demand as much or be reciprocated as much, so spontaneously. There is no one I know who could exact such self-discipline and dedication and at the same time receive so much love.

Her greatness as a teacher lay not only in these basic human qualities, but also in the fact that she herself had a musical ear that

was beyond belief; later, when she was almost blind, this ability became if anything even more acute and specific. She heard and knew exactly what she heard.

Nadia had a combination of the most rigorous French intellectual clarity and a wonderful Russian abandon and generosity, so very un-French in its boundless exuberance.

I have made music with Nadia Boulanger regularly over many years at my Festival in Bath and at the Festival now in its twenty-fourth year in Gstaad. We played chamber music; she played the piano; she conducted; she brought her choir; she accompanied me in the Stravinsky Violin Concerto in London. You can imagine how eager I was that our youngest and most musical son, Jeremy, should benefit from Nadia's influence. Promptly, in her generous way, she had him to live in her apartment in Paris when he was fifteen. Thus he was under her aegis daily, receiving her guidance in the matter of composition, and to some extent with regard to the piano.

She always remained deeply devout, and was a Roman Catholic. Perhaps that, and the fact that she always dressed somewhat severely in black or grey, was misleading: she was always open-minded and entirely youthful in her acceptance of the new, provided that it stood up critically to norms and standards which were timeless in themselves. To her, the particular style of a work was of no account, so long as each note fitted into the scheme of things and had a message to give and met with her proviso: that the composer could hear what he was writing while he was composing it, and that consequently it was unmistakably his own, sincere voice.

Jeremy Menuhin

My relationship with Nadia was definitely a special one. Ever since I can remember, my wish was to be a musician, but at eleven it had become a decision. This decision was not encouraged, and I was sent to Eton in the hope that I would be a British gentleman rather than another wandering musician. A rare opportunity to display my musical aptitude occurred when Nadia was visiting our house in Switzerland. It was she who, despite my family, was responsible for my going to Paris to study music; she echoed my wish for music by expressing faith in me.

For two years I lived in a room above her flat, and shared both lunch and supper with her almost every day. Inevitably this led to the discussion of many subjects, excluding religion and politics, which Nadia considered too personal to broach. However the subject of my changing voice did not seem too personal, as one day, Nadia expressed concern that my voice should still be so high-pitched, considering my fifteen years. I replied that it was none of her business, as in those days it was easier to be blunt. She heaved a sigh and said, 'I thought I was more than just a professor. . .'. It was a rare admission of vulnerability, and left me feeling miserable though still defensive. The next day I arrived at my lesson determined to maintain a low growl and never to revert to my 'falsetto'. Indeed, from then on, my voice remained at a level about two octaves lower. Nadia pretended to notice nothing.

Nadia Boulanger with Jeremy Menuhin and Oleg Markevitch (left)

Murray Perahia

I was never her pupil, but I first met Mademoiselle Boulanger when she judged the Leeds Piano Competition in 1972. She had bent the rules about the jury talking to competitors, and spoke to me about my playing and asked about my background. When I told her I was an American, she said that was impossible, that she herself was not exclusively French and felt that her Russian background was important. She was insistent that I call her when I was in Paris, which I later did, but because of her very busy teaching schedule we couldn't arrange a meeting in time.

I also remember sending her my first recording (it was Schumann's *Davidsbundler-Tanze*, Op.6), and through a student she told me that while she enjoyed it, there were three or four places where she distinctly heard the music differently; alas, I was never to find out what they were.

Eventually we did have a meeting, and it came about more unexpectedly. I was in Paris playing the Chopin concerto in a series of concerts with the Orchestre de Paris. Minutes before I was to go onstage for the last performance (a Sunday morning), I received a letter from Mademoiselle Boulanger, delivered by hand, saying how sorry she was that she had to 'sacrifice' hearing me, but because of infirmities she couldn't go out. When I finished playing, I immediately called her and, after exchanging cordialities, she asked when I was going back to London. I had planned to go pretty soon, but told her that I could change it so I could visit her. She seemed pleased and told me to come over for an hour. It was then that I saw the dimly-lit room with the old furniture and fittings that I had heard so much about. She sat in a corner, somewhat shrivelled, not as upright as I had remembered her at Leeds, but very vibrant and her mind active. We spoke of many things: first she asked me my repertoire and advised me to play more modern music. She spoke very warmly of Copland's Variations, which she said was like a rock, solid as granite. She then talked about Schumann, how much she loved his music — but that she often found it being played too quickly — one couldn't hear the harmonious shifts when it went by so rapidly. But then she said there was no such thing as the *right* tempo, it was a question of the interpreter 'understanding' the piece. To demonstrate this, she played (with a rather trembling left hand) a fugue subject of Bach. I am still awed by the rhythm and character with which she imbued it when I recollect that experience. She told me she felt sure of that tempo until she heard Richter play it much slower (and she demonstrated that).

One thing she said that was very touching, and somewhat sad when I remember it, involved her feeling about herself as a teacher. She felt that the basis — the real basis — of music, the heartfelt love for it, the most immediate response to it, was something unteachable. And what she taught was what the real musician would feel a need to learn himself, or could learn by himself once that immediate response was there. This innate instinct for music was more important to her than all the academic theories. Actually, I feel that is a tribute to her own innate and all-consuming love of music.

It was the last time I ever saw her, and I will long cherish that exhilarating hour with her.

Pierre Schaeffer: the Statue of Liberty

In trying to evoke the personality of Nadia Boulanger, an image occurs to me. I ask forgiveness for its preposterous not to say off-hand nature. Well, here it is — since the statue of Liberty whose silhouette has long dominated the shipping around it reigns over the harbour of New York, I am permitting myself to set up the Great Lady of my memory in like manner as the last sign of my wanderings, the ultimate vigil of my uncertain vagabondage.

First of all, her stature: greater than ours and, furthermore, rising up beside the piano so that she could keep on the horizon of her singers. Initial vision then of Nadia Boulanger conducting the Cantata whose code number I have never ceased to chase, in the way a sailor gets his bearings from degrees of longitude and latitude. I knew it once and it will recur to me but, for the moment, it slips my memory. What lingers in my ears, however, is the interplay of the voices, fingertips on the keyboard, the German words, the Paris salon, the Slavonic fervour — in other words the whole general effect (the American 'melting-pot'). At all events, the Bach Cantata in all its pitiless, irrefutable, unchallengeable brilliance — the torch held at arm's length at the top of the Statue.

To fix this definitive vision two other settings, two other actions are required. One, earlier and provincial, happened in Lorraine in the cramped ambience of conservatoire-type music, in a humble display of family musicianship. I was indeed familiar with the repertoire, having heard it thumped out by my parents' pupils, gone through it in insecure performances in the end-of-the-year competitions, finally having dreaded it when my parents performed themselves. The music was now a display of painful pedagogy, now an unashamed contest or a cruel trial in which my parents were risking if not their lives at least their reputation and, in particular, being considered top-class by me. I still have not recovered from the memory of those exhibitions.

I had also served my apprenticeship in those contests reserved for the categories of my youthful age, groaned over my 'cello, done my drudgery on the pianoforte, triumphed in solfeggio exercises since I was able to guess all the notes with my eyes closed. In short, I had served as a cabin-boy on a drifter and became as familiar with its lockers as with the disasters from which, in my turn, I had managed to extricate myself. Yet never had I set eyes on the majesty of the great port nor perceived the splendour of the illuminated seaboard of a whole continent. All this the Great Lady had revealed to me instantaneously — the ocean from which I emerged like a poor mariner, the fertile lands of genius and the profusion of light which reigned over all. If I had been Nadia Boulanger's worst pupil, I certainly proved to be the quickest: in two hours of cantata I believe I had grasped everything.

I could embellish the theme, state what I understood then and what has never ceased to haunt and persecute me in my own struggles. A conception of music, so sublime, so severe, yet at the same time so tender and protective as to be almost unbearable. How then, after all these allusions, can I explain my own wanderings? A saying of Hoffmann's has helped me to throw light on them: 'sound dwells everywhere; but sounds, I mean the melodies that speak the superior language of the kingdom of the mind, dwell only in man's heart'. So, to continue the metaphor, I avoided the port and trusted myself to this solitary raft, borne away far from the shore by treacherous currents. Sometimes a lighthouse in the fog reminded me of my point of departure. Hermann Scherchen, he too, lonely in his quest, was one such beacon. His name is associated in my mind with that of Nadia Boulanger, strangely different from her but belonging to the same constellation.

Whereas I could at times relate my drifting to the Scherchen landmarks, there was never any question of my rediscovering Nadia Boulanger in this way. As a friend, certainly, thanks to tricks of memory and habits of fidelity in which she herself was the virtuoso, but not as a musician. Profound discretion, modesty of silence. Although I never tackled her on the question, I allow myself to believe she had some opinion of me, perhaps based simply on the promise she saw in me at twenty-five. It is the secret that still binds us, and for ever. Painful though it is to me and at the risk of offending the reader, I will pursue my image to the end. So, remorselessly, I come to the final image, that of the *Planet of the Apes* — a film which I consider a masterpiece as a pitiless fable, but certainly not one for children. After their voyage in Time-Space the Earth Cosmonauts are shipwrecked on their own planet. Where their port was they find nothing but sand, nothing but a severed head, the ultimate gesture of a lifeless torch. I leave in doubt this equivocal truth that our Masters have foundered or that our children are lost.

Paul Valéry

Music is not my profession. I respond to it strongly in certain works, but after my own fashion, which is not reliable. So I cannot speak of Mademoiselle Boulanger's technical merits. But I have watched her at work often enough: standing in her long black pleated skirts; her face pale, as though spellbound, the occasional gleam of light from her spectacles; one hand playing the piano, the other directing with a finger the little orchestra fanned around her.

Nadia conducts. One might say that she exhales what one hears, and that she does not and could not exist except in the universe of sound.

Even someone as ignorant as I am retains an extraordinary impression. Before one's eyes a living creature produces enthusiasm and order, which are the two symmetrical powers of great art. But these two major virtues of performance — as they are of all creation — do not harmonize except through discipline

and sustained practice, which transforms their antagonism into equilibrium. One does nothing good without passion; nothing excellent by passion alone. Nadia Boulanger seems to me infused with some principle analogous to this. The joy of comprehending, the willingness to make comprehensible, are joined in her with a determination not to sacrifice a work's structure to local effects, precision to the advantages of approximation, purity to the individual intentions of the interpreter. Ingres, in his energetic and bizarre language, used to say — speaking of drawing — 'You must risk your neck even for a study'. Nadia Boulanger might say so for the beat, I think.

I have talked with her frequently. I think we understand each other quite well. There is a philosophy of performance which dominates all the arts, which allows us to exchange ideas born of action rather than intention, of experience rather than discussion. In the course of these conversations, Mademoiselle Boulanger has sometimes allowed me the illusion that I understand something of the subtleties and skilful arrangement of great Music . . .

from *La Revue Internationale de la Musique*, October–November 1938.

Chronology

1887   16 September. Nadia Boulanger born in Paris. Family of musicians: grandmother, Juliette Boulanger, a celebrated singer; father, Ernest Boulanger, professor at the Paris Conservatoire de Musique and composer. Mother of Russian origin, née Princess Mitchesky.

1893   Birth of Lili Boulanger.

1897   Enters the Paris Conservatoire.

1900   Death of Ernest Boulanger.

1904   First prizes in harmony, counterpoint, organ, fugue, and piano accompaniment.

1906   Assistant to Henri Dallier at the great organ of the Madeleine Church.

1908   Deuxième Grand Prix de Rome. Composes and gives a number of concerts.

1910   Writes *La Ville Morte* in collaboration with Raoul Pugno, with a libretto by d'Annunzio.
       Devotes herself to teaching.

1908–1918   Takes the harmony class at the Conservatoire (1913: Lili Boulanger wins Premier Grand Prix de Rome).

1918   15 March. Death of Lili Boulanger.

1921   Professor of the Conservatoire Américain at Fontainebleau. Provides classes there in harmony, counterpoint and composition until her death. Teaches at the Ecole Normale de Musique (harmony, counterpoint, composition, history of music), first as assistant to Paul Dukas, then as full Professor until 1939.
       First tour of the United States, to which she frequently returned, giving concerts, classes and lectures.

1940–46   Long stay in the United States, conducts the Boston Symphony Orchestra and the New York Symphony Orchestra.

1946–57   Professor of piano accompaniment at the Conservatoire National supérieur de musique de Paris.

1950   Appointed Director of the Conservatoire Américain at Fontainebleau.

1979   22 October. Nadia Boulanger died in Paris.
       Throughout her career she gave numerous concerts and lectures both in France and abroad, at the same time giving private lessons to innumerable pupils of all nationalities.

Discography

Recordings made by Nadia Boulanger for HMV (78 rpm).
1937
Monteverdi: *Madrigals* (Reissued by HMV; Helios)

Françaix: *Concerto for piano and orchestra*
with the Orchestre Philharmonique de Paris
directed by Nadia Boulanger

1938
Brahms: *Liebes Liederwalzer*
with Marie-Blanche de Polignac, Doda Conrad
Piano duet: Nadia Boulanger
            Dinu Lipatti

Brahms: *Waltzes*
Piano duet: Nadia Boulanger
            Dinu Lipatti

Brahms: *Duets for Female voices*
with Nathalie and Irène Kedroff, Marie-Blanche de Polignac
Piano: Nadia Boulanger

Schubert: *Mondschein*
with Paul Derenne, vocal ensemble
Piano: Nadia Boulanger

1948
Fauré: *Requiem* (Reissued by EMI)
Gisèle Peyron, soprano
Doda Conrad, baritone
Maurice Duruflé, organ
Chorale Yvonne Gouverne
Orchestre Philharmonique de Paris
Directed by Nadia Boulanger

Recordings for Boite à Musique and recently reissued by Turnabout

Petit Concert, a collection of works by Fauré, Debussy, Lili
Boulanger etc . . .
with Gisèle Peyron, Paul Derenne, Marie-Thérèse Holley,
Doda Conrad

Recordings made in Paris for Gold Seal Decca U.S.A. in 1950 (33 rpm)

Monteverdi: *Madrigals* (2nd series)
with Gisèle Peyron, Marie-Thérèse Holley, Paul Derenne, Doda Conrad
Orchestre Philharmonique de Paris
Directed by Nadia Boulanger

M.-A. Charpentier: *Médée*
with Paul Derenne, Gisèle Peyron, Irma Collassy, Doda Conrad, Marie-Thérèse Holley
Orchestre Philharmonique de Paris
Directed by Nadia Boulanger

Rameau: *Operas* (extracts): *Dardanus, Hippolyte* and *Aricie*, etc
the same singers and the Chorale Yvonne Gouverne
Orchestre Philharmonique de Paris
Directed by Nadia Boulanger

Renaissance française
A capella (same singers)

Brahms: *Liebes Liederwalzer*
      Seven Quartets for Voices
Flora Wend, Nancy Waugh, Hugues Cuenod, Doda Conrad
Piano duet: Nadia Boulanger
          Jean Françaix

Index